THE BOOK OF
GOLF
LISTS

Edited by Norman Giller

TREASURE PRESS

First published in Great Britain in 1985 by
Sidgwick & Jackson Limited

This edition published in 1988 by
Treasure Press
59 Grosvenor Street
London W1

Copyright © 1985 Norman Giller

Picture research: Malcolm Rowley

ISBN 1 85051 282 5

Printed in Czechoslovakia
50665

This book is dedicated to the memory of
Ronald Heager, a golf journalist of the highest order
who helped show me the course to take when we were
together in the same *Daily Express* team.

CONTENTS

SECTION FOUR: All Kinds of Everything

SECTION FIVE: Just Amazing   129

SECTION SIX: All About the Open

SECTION SEVEN: The Complete List of Champions   178

ACKNOWLEDGEMENTS

I wish to thank the compilers of the following books which were top of my list for reference checks:

The *Benson and Hedges Golfer's Handbook 1984* (Macmillan, in association with *Golf Monthly*); various previous annual editions of the *Golfer's Handbook*; various annual editions of *World of Golf* (Macdonald and Jane's); *The Story of the Open Golf Championship, 1860–1950* by Charles G. Mortimer and Fred Pignon (Jarrolds); *The Open* by Peter Alliss with Michael Hobbs (Collins); *Golf, A Pictorial History* by Henry Cotton (Collins); various annual editions of *The World of Professional Golf* by Mark H. McCormack (Springwood Books); *Royal and Ancient Championship Records, 1860–1980;* and the always informative magazines *Golf Monthly, Golfer's Companion, Golf Illustrated,* and *Golf World.*

Thanks also to the officials of the U.S. and European PGAs, the United States Golf Association and, above all, the Royal and Ancient Golf Club of St Andrews for their kind co-operation. I would also like to express my gratitude to photographer Phil Sheldon for providing all the pictures that are featured, Malcolm Rowley for his diligent research, computer wizard Michael Carter for showing me that an Apple a day keeps the bank manager away; and also to Sidgwick and Jackson's dynamic duo Margaret Willes and Carey Smith for their encouragement and professionalism.

Most of all I wish to thank the many international golfers who took time out to answer my irritating questions. They have between them given the book an authority it might otherwise have lacked. In return for their co-operation I am making a donation to the Children In Need Fund.

NORMAN GILLER

THE FIRST TEE
Introduction by Norman Giller

Many of the world's leading golfers have helped me in the compilation of this *Book of Golf Lists* that hopefully will stimulate debates and discussions at the nineteenth hole and beyond. It is as much a book about *feelings* as facts, with the expert opinions of a panel of top golfing personalities giving a foundation of authority to diligently researched records, statistics and events.

My objective on the following pages is to entertain as well as enlighten with the most varied collection of golf lists ever collated in one volume. There are:

COMPUTERIZED RATINGS of the all-time great champions.
An **OPEN OPINION POLL** in which more than 1,000 views on golf have been analysed.
Exclusive personalized **STARFILES** by a galaxy of great golfers including six winners of the British Open championship.
A **MILLION DOLLAR LEAGUE TABLE** giving the career earnings of sixty of the most successful players in the world.
A **'JUST AMAZING'** section featuring dozens of incredible golfing facts.
Twenty-five **WINNING WOMEN OF GOLF**, proving that Mrs Worthington would be better advised to put her daughter on the tee rather than the stage.
A complete list of the world's **MAJOR CHAMPIONSHIP** winners.

Whether you are a tiger or, like me, a rabbit you will find facts in this book that will inform, amuse and, occasionally, bemuse you. You are likely to have any set opinions you may hold on golf severely tested and challenged when you read what the experts think about the game's personalities and performances.

My work on this book was made considerably easier by the cooperation of many golfers from around the world and in return for their participation I am making a donation to the Children In Need Fund.

I have a feeling many of the lists will start more arguments than they settle, but I am sure that whether you go straight down the middle of the book or pitch in at any page you will find plenty to arouse your interest. Now it's your honour, so off you go...

SECTION ONE
THE GREATEST OF THE GREATS

THE GOLFERS' GOLFERS

In a bid to settle the never-ending argument as to who have been the greatest golfers of the century we fed all the facts and figures on the leading contenders into a computer. We then added the *feelings* expressed by the dozens of top golfers, past and present, who kindly gave us their opinions based on their experiences. More than one hundred players were separated into pre-war and post-war groups and we took into account not only tournament victories but also the overall impact they have made on the international golf circuit. This is how the 'Top Ten' giants of golf were computer rated:

MODERN MASTERS (1945–)

1 **JACK NICKLAUS** *(USA)*
2 **BEN HOGAN** *(USA)*
3 **TOM WATSON** *(USA)*
4 **ARNOLD PALMER** *(USA)*
5 **GARY PLAYER** *(South Africa)*
6 **LEE TREVINO** *(USA)*
7 **SAM SNEAD** *(USA)*
8 **SEVE BALLESTEROS** *(Spain)*
9 **PETER THOMSON** *(Australia)*
10 **BOBBY LOCKE** *(South Africa)*

GOLDEN OLDIES (1900–1945)

1 **BOBBY JONES** *(USA)*
2 **WALTER HAGEN** *(USA)*
3 **HARRY VARDON** *(Great Britain)*
4 **GENE SARAZEN** *(USA)*
5 **BYRON NELSON** *(USA)*
6 **HENRY COTTON** *(Great Britain)*
7 **TOMMY ARMOUR** *(USA)*
8 **JAMES BRAID** *(Great Britain)*
9 **JOHN HENRY TAYLOR** *(Great Britain)*
10 **TED RAY** *(Great Britain)*

Jack Nicklaus...the Modern Master

STARFILE No. 1

GARY PLAYER
My Idea of the Ten Greatest Golfers

1 **JACK NICKLAUS** *(USA)*
2 **ARNOLD PALMER** *(USA)*
3 **LEE TREVINO** *(USA)*
4 **SAM SNEAD** *(USA)*
5 **BEN HOGAN** *(USA)*
6 **GENE SARAZEN** *(USA)*
7 **TOM WATSON** *(USA)*
8 **SEVE BALLESTEROS** *(Spain)*
9 **BOBBY JONES** *(USA)*
10 **BOBBY LOCKE** *(South Africa)*

'This is the order in which they came to mind and not how I necessarily rate them. I am proud to have my fellow South African Bobby Locke in the list. Not only was he a fine player but he was also a great inspiration to me when I was a youngster and he was among the people who encouraged me to travel the world to improve my game.'

MY BOYHOOD GOLFING HEROES: The three players who captured my imagination when I first started to take up the game were Bobby Jones, Byron Nelson and Ben Hogan. All are legendary figures in the game and I used to get a big kick reading about their exploits.

MY MOST MEMORABLE TOURNAMENT: It has to be the U.S. Open at the Bellerive Country Club, St Louis, in 1965. It was played in tremendous heat and humidity and I kept myself going with lots of honey. An overseas player had not won the title for forty-five years and what made it particularly significant for me is that my victory after a play-off with Kel Nagle made me only the third golfer in history to complete the Grand Slam. Ben Hogan and Gene Sarazen were the only golfers who had been there before me. I had the satisfaction of being able to hand back the winner's $25,000 cheque for donation to cancer research and to help promote junior golf. The title and the Grand Slam were sufficient reward for me.

12

THE GREATEST CHAMPIONSHIP-WINNING PERFORM-ANCE: The one that stands out in my memory is the victory by Jack Nicklaus in the U.S. Masters at Augusta in 1965. Jack was just untouchable. He equalled Lloyd Mangrum's record individual round with a third-round 64 and lowered the all-time best aggregate to 271. Arnold Palmer and I tied for second place on 280.

THE SPORTSMAN I MOST ADMIRE OUTSIDE GOLF: Bjorn Borg, because he was so humble and well behaved when at his peak and gave the perfect example of how a great champion should conduct himself.

FOR THE RECORD

GARY PLAYER stands only 5 foot 7 inches but is a golfing giant when measured by his ability and achievements. A professional since the age of eighteen, this fitness fanatic has been challenging for the world's major prizes for more than twenty years. He is a powerful and accurate player and, above all, a determined competitor who never admits defeat until the final putt has dropped. Gary, born in Lyndhurst, Johannesburg, in 1935, has won more than 120 principal events during his globe-trotting career including three Open championships, three Masters titles, the U.S. Open once, the U.S. PGA championship twice, eleven South African Open titles, seven Australian Open titles and five World Match Play championships. Early in his career Gary asked a seasoned British professional for an opinion on his play and was told quite bluntly: 'Go home, young man, and get yourself an honest job.' A God-fearing man whose behaviour on and off the golf course has always been exemplary, Gary ignored the advice and practised, practised and practised until he had developed his game out of all recognition. The way he has worked at his game to manufacture himself into one of the greatest golfers of all time is an inspiration to anybody not born with natural sporting skills.

STARFILE No. 2

BILL ROGERS
My Magnificent Seven

1 **JACK NICKLAUS** *(USA)*
2 **BEN HOGAN** *(USA)*
3 **TOM WATSON** *(USA)*
4 **SEVE BALLESTEROS** *(Spain)*
5 **ARNOLD PALMER** *(USA)*
6 **GARY PLAYER** *(South Africa)*
7 **JOHNNY MILLER** *(USA)*

'These are, in my opinion, the seven greatest golfers of my lifetime. You only have to look in the record books to find plenty of evidence to back my judgement. All of them are masters of golf who both by their skill and their conduct are a credit to the game.'

MY BOYHOOD GOLFING HEROES: Arnold Palmer was at his peak when I first became aware of the great game of golf and during my teens Jack Nicklaus started to get into his stride. These were the two heroes I looked up to and it was a great thrill to play with them when I joined the professional circuit.

MY MOST MEMORABLE TOURNAMENT: How can I ever forget the British Open at Royal St George's in 1981! It was my first major championship and I had the tremendous satisfaction of stepping on the eighteenth tee on the final day with a four-shot lead. It was one of those championships when everything went right and I was the only competitor who had a below-par aggregate score for the seventy-two holes. I will always remember the extraordinary sights and sounds as I walked down the final fairway with the enormous grandstands packed with applauding spectators. The moment I hit my approach shot towards the flag the crowd rushed on to the fairway to get a good view of the eighteenth green. As I threaded my way through the spectators a policeman shoved me in the chest and pushed me back. 'Take it easy, pal,' I told him. 'I'm just trying to finish!'

THE GREATEST CHAMPIONSHIP-WINNING PERFORM-ANCE: I have never known a more exciting finish than that to the U.S. Masters in 1975. Jack Nicklaus held off a storming finish by Tom Weiskopf and Johnny Miller to clinch his record fifth victory. Both Weiskopf and Miller had chances of birdies at the seventy-second hole to force a play-off with Nicklaus but each missed fairly short putts. Miller had really burned up the course on the first nine with a 30 that included six successive birdies. Nicklaus shot 68−67−73−68 for an aggregate 276 and victory by one stroke from Miller and Weiskopf.

THE SPORTSMAN I MOST ADMIRE OUTSIDE GOLF: Bjorn Borg was the sportsman I have always admired. He was the professionals' professional whose approach to his sport set an example for all sportsmen. Borg was not only an exceptional player but also carried himself with dignity in victory and defeat.

FOR THE RECORD

BILL ROGERS is a lanky, genial Texan who captured the hearts of all British golf followers with his pleasant personality when he emerged as the surprise winner of the Open at Royal St George's in 1981. Early in that memorable season he had missed the cut five times in seven starts but his game picked up after he had won the Sea Pines Heritage Classic and he followed a second place in the U.S. Open by winning at St George's and then coming out top in the World Series Golf, the Texas Open, the Suntory Open in Japan, the New South Wales Open and the Australian Open. He laid the foundation to his career in college golf and won the 1972 Southern Amateur and the 1973 All-American Collegiate titles. One of his most impressive performances before his Open triumph came in the 1980 Suntory World Match Play championship at Wentworth in 1980 when he conquered Isao Aoki in the final. Bill, born in Waco, Texas, in 1951, has a smooth, flat swing that reminds many experienced golf followers of another Texan — Ben Hogan. There can be no higher praise.

STARFILE No. 3

BERNHARD LANGER
The Five Greatest Drivers

1 **GREG NORMAN** *(Australia)*
2 **JACK NICKLAUS** *(USA)*
3 **LANNY WADKINS** *(USA)*
4 **SEVE BALLESTEROS** *(Spain)*
5 **Dr GIL MORGAN** *(USA)*

'They can all unleash the big, powerhouse drive and are always long and usually pretty straight. If you had asked for the top six drivers I would have included myself because I pride myself on being able to hit a good long drive!'

MY BOYHOOD GOLFING HEROES: There were two players who held my interest above all others – Gary Player and Jack Nicklaus. I admired their attitude and consistency and, of course, their command of all aspects of the game. It was an ambition achieved for me when I played in the same tournaments as these two wonderful golfing ambassadors.

MY MOST MEMORABLE TOURNAMENT: It has to be my victory in the 1985 U.S. Masters on that wonderful course in Augusta. I kept plugging away and managed to overhaul Curtis Strange over the last nine holes when it seemed at one time that he could not be caught. It was the proudest moment of my career when 1984 Masters champion Ben Crenshaw helped me on with the famous green jacket. The tournament that has given me most pleasure in Europe is the British Open at Royal St George's in 1981. I was runner-up to Bill Rogers and it was great for me to be in contention for the title. There was one stage on the final day when I pulled back to within one stroke of Bill, who had started the round with a four-stroke advantage. I recall rolling in a 60-foot putt for a birdie at the sixteenth on the final round, but Bill continued to play steadily and finally won with four shots to spare. What thrilled me was to be so warmly welcomed and cheered on by the British spectators. They made me feel very much at home.

THE GREATEST CHAMPIONSHIP-WINNING PERFORM-ANCE: There has surely not been a more exciting or better quality head-to-head duel than that between Jack Nicklaus and Tom Watson in the British Open at Turnberry in 1977. Both were playing at their very best and their respective cards provide proof of their excellence – Watson: 68–70–65–65 for a record 268; Nicklaus 68–70–65–66 for a 269. *Wunderbar!*

THE SPORTSMAN I MOST ADMIRE OUTSIDE GOLF: Bjorn Borg was the sportsman I considered head and shoulders above all others for ability and attitude. Even when under the severest pressure he was able to show incredible concentration and composure.

FOR THE RECORD

BERNHARD LANGER has almost single-handedly started a golfing revolution in West Germany where his success on the golf courses of the world has triggered a booming interest in the game. Bernhard is not only one of the longest hitters on the circuit but is also one of the most accurate shot-makers. His growing list of triumphs would be even more impressive but for his unpredictability on the putting green where he is either hopeless or brilliant with no apparent in-between form. Born in Anhousen in 1957, he gave the world notice of his potential when, almost unknown, he led the South American Order of Merit in 1979. The following year in the Dunlop Masters he became the first German to win a European Tour event and in 1981 he finished runner-up to Bill Rogers in the Open at Royal St George's. He showed remarkable consistency throughout 1981, competing in seventeen events and finishing in the top ten on fourteen occasions. Leading from start to finish, he became the first German to take his country's Open championship with an impressive 67–69–64–72 sequence. He captured his first major championship at Augusta in April 1985, when he chopped back what had looked an unassailable lead held by Curtis Strange to win the U.S. Masters. It cemented Bernhard's place in the front rank of world golfers.

STARFILE No. 4

JOHNNY MILLER
MY IDENTIKIT OF THE 'PERFECT' GOLFER

The **DRIVING POWER** and **ACCURACY** of **GREG NORMAN**
The **LONG IRON SHOTS** of **JACK NICKLAUS**
The **SHORT GAME** of **TOM WATSON**
The **BUNKER SHOTS** of **GARY PLAYER**
The **PUTTING** of **TOM WATSON**
The **TEMPERAMENT** of **BOBBY LOCKE**

'If you could put all these attributes together you would have the "perfect" golfer. My idea of the player who has come closest to perfection is Ben Hogan, a boyhood hero of mine who mastered all the shots and had great courage and character to go with his talent.'

MY BOYHOOD GOLFING HEROES: Ben Hogan, Cary Middlecoff and Tony Lema shared my affection and admiration when I was first attracted to the great game of golf. Hogan is, of course, a golfing legend whose feats on and off the course are well recorded. Cary Middlecoff was known as 'Doc' because he was a qualified dentist. He was twice U.S. Open champion and won the Masters in 1955. Tony Lema had lots of style and a great personality as was evidenced in his nickname 'Champagne Tony'. He was tragically killed in a plane crash when at his peak.

MY MOST MEMORABLE TOURNAMENT: It has to be my victory in the U.S. Open at Oakmont in 1973. I began with a 71 and a 69 but then looked as if I had thrown away my chances when I returned a 76 for the third round. Going into the final round I trailed Palmer, Boros, Schlee and Heard by six strokes. I started the last eighteen holes with four successive birdies and this brought me back into contention and gave me the confidence to go for my shots. I added five more birdies and was home in 63 for the lowest closing round in any major championship. It gave me an aggregate of 279 and victory by one stroke from John Schlee with Arnold Palmer and Tom Weiskopf a further stroke behind in joint third place.

THE GREATEST CHAMPIONSHIP-WINNING PERFORM-ANCE: Sorry, but I have to go for my 1973 U.S. Open victory again. My final eighteen holes produced one of those rounds you dream about. I started out an hour before the leaders and there seemed no way back into the hunt for me. But you can hardly do better than open with four birdies, and suddenly, instead of being six strokes adrift, I was breathing down the necks of the leading players. I hit every fairway and, with nothing to lose, went for the flag with my irons. I made some pretty good putts but also missed a few, otherwise my round of 63 would have been even better.

THE SPORTSMAN I MOST ADMIRE OUTSIDE GOLF: Wayne Gretzky, the sharp and skilled ice hockey star who, in only his third year in the league with the Edmonton Oilers in 1981−82, demolished all the National Hockey League records. He scored 92 goals and had a record 120 assists.

FOR THE RECORD

JOHNNY MILLER was being hailed as the 'new' Jack Nicklaus in the 1970s when he lit up the golf courses of the world with some scintillating play. 'King Jack' was, of course, in no mood to vacate his throne but there was certainly a time when Johnny looked as good as any player to have stepped on a tee. Coached by his father, Johnny made an early impact when he won the U.S. Junior championship in 1964. He joined the professional circuit in 1969 and within a year was fortieth on the U.S. Tour. In 1971 he won his first premier event, the Southern Open, and by 1977 he had raised his championship collection to seventeen titles before hitting an inexplicable slump. The tall, blond, well-mannered Mormon, born in San Francisco in 1949, touched an Everest peak in 1974 when he captured nine trophies and set a then U.S. money-earning record of $353,021. His greatest moment came in the U.S. Open in 1973 when he clinched the championship with an astonishing final round of 63. He added the British Open to his honours haul at Royal Birkdale in 1976, this time with a final round of 66 to hold off the challenge of a young nineteen-year-old gladiator called Severiano Ballesteros.

Johnny Miller...hailed as the new king

Seve Ballesteros...the most exciting golfer in the world

STARFILE No. 5

SEVE BALLESTEROS
The Ten Greatest Golfers of My Lifetime

1   **JACK NICKLAUS** *(USA)*
2   **SAM SNEAD** *(USA)*
3   **GARY PLAYER** *(South Africa)*
4   **LEE TREVINO** *(USA)*
5   **ARNOLD PALMER** *(USA)*
6   **TOM WATSON** *(USA)*
7   **ROBERTO DE VICENZO** *(Argentina)*
8   **BILLY CASPER** *(USA)*
9   **JOHNNY MILLER** *(USA)*
10 **GREG NORMAN** *(Australia)*

'It was very difficult compiling this list but the one fact about which I had no doubt is that Jack Nicklaus has to be Number One. Nicklaus has a record that speaks for itself. His consistency is just amazing and I truly admire his dedication and commitment.'

MY BOYHOOD GOLFING HEROES: Jack Nicklaus, Lee Trevino and Gary Player were my boyhood heroes outside Spain and it has given me immense pleasure to play in the same tournaments as them. They have always lived up to the picture I had of them in my mind when I was a youngster first learning to love golf.

MY MOST MEMORABLE TOURNAMENT: Two share an equal place in my memory – the British Open championships of 1979 and 1984 both of which I was privileged to win. My victory at Royal Lytham in 1979 was perhaps the most memorable because it was my first major championship victory and I managed to make some pretty good recovery shots after hitting only two fairways with my driver in the last two rounds. I had not been playing well going into the 1984 Open at St Andrews but I found my form and had the satisfaction of beating defending champion Tom Watson and Bernhard Langer by two strokes to take the championship. It was a tremendous feeling to sink a fifteen-foot putt for a birdie on the last green.

THE GREATEST CHAMPIONSHIP-WINNING PERFORM-ANCE: Gary Player's astonishing victory in the U.S. Masters at Augusta in 1978. It was his third Masters triumph and it came seventeen years after his first. Only as positive a person as Gary would have given himself a chance when he went into the final round seven strokes behind the leader, Hubert Green. He had seven birdies on the last seven holes for a record last-round 64 and victory by one stroke.

THE SPORTSMAN I MOST ADMIRE OUTSIDE GOLF: I was always a great fan of Muhammad Ali's. There was no other heavyweight anywhere near his class when he was at his peak. He used to say that he was 'The Greatest' and then provide action to go with his words.

FOR THE RECORD

SEVE BALLESTEROS has in a few short years established himself as the most exciting golfer in the world; certainly the most dynamic player since Arnold Palmer was at his peak. The son of a Spanish farmer, Seve was born into a golf-crazy family. His uncle, Ramon Sota, was a top-class international player, and he followed two brothers into professional golf after spending hours of his boyhood caddying and learning to master the game at every spare second. By the time he was twenty-three, Seve had won the Open championship and the U.S. Masters; finished first in his debut tournament in the United States; headed the European Order of Merit three times; helped Spain win the World Cup twice and won six consecutive tournaments in the U.K., U.S.A., Europe, East Africa, Japan and New Zealand. There were mutterings midway through 1984 that he had touched his peak and was on the downhill run but he then provided more evidence to prove he has become a true giant of the game by winning the Open in a thrilling photofinish with five-times champion Tom Watson. Seve is young enough and good enough to challenge one day his idol Jack Nicklaus for the mantle of the finest golfer of modern times.

STARFILE No. 6

TOMMY HORTON
The Six Greatest Short-Game Artists

1 **BOBBY LOCKE** *(South Africa)*
A supreme wedge player and putter
2 **GARY PLAYER** *(South Africa)*
Plays all short shots well by attacking everything
3 **TOM WATSON** *(USA)*
A clever and inventive wedge player and a marvellous putter
4 **BILLY CASPER** *(USA)*
He was brilliant at getting out of bunkers and was a deadly putter
5 **BOB CHARLES** *(New Zealand)*
'Mr Reliable' anywhere near the green and with the putter in his hand
6 **SEVE BALLESTEROS** *(Spain)*
A true artist no matter which club he's holding in his hand

'Seve Ballesteros is the most gifted of them all. He has a natural, instinctive "feel" for the game and has the best understanding of the spin of the ball.'

MY BOYHOOD GOLFING HEROES: Three grabbed my attention: Henry Cotton, who had an iron nerve and wonderful striking ability...Max Faulkner, who was colourful and exciting and had the sweetest of swings...Ben Hogan, whose cold nerve and sheer determination lifted him above his rivals.

MY MOST MEMORABLE TOURNAMENT: The 1978 Dunlop Masters at St Pierre takes pride of place for me. There was a world-class field of professionals competing and I managed to clinch the championship with an eight-foot putt on the last green for an aggregate total of 279. One of the most marvellous moments of my career was shared by thousands of enthusiastic spectators and the TV cameras were in attendance. It was particularly memorable for me because the prestigious win came in what was my year as PGA captain.

THE GREATEST CHAMPIONSHIP-WINNING PERFORM-ANCE: Tom Watson's one-stroke victory over Jack Nicklaus in the 1977 Open made the Turnberry championship one of the greatest classics of all time. The two finest golfers in the world battled it out over the last two rounds and their scoring spread-eagled the field. I had managed a third-round 65 but could not live with the pace being set by Watson and Nicklaus and finally finished highest-placed British competitor in ninth place. Watson's short-game was absolutely inspired over the vital last nine holes and the determination of Nicklaus with his final shot to the green and then his last putt was just phenomenal. He did not give up until the final putt had dropped. It was magical stuff by both of these golfing greats.

THE SPORTSMAN I MOST ADMIRE OUTSIDE GOLF: Bjorn Borg was, for me, The King. He was never ever flustered, had great patience and possessed powers of concentration that were quite awesome. His unique combination of faultless technique and mental strength made him the best player in the world and his conduct on and off the court meant he was a wonderful ambassador for his sport and his country.

FOR THE RECORD

TOMMY HORTON has been a prominent player on the European circuit for a span of two decades since launching his tournament career in 1964. A respected teacher and resident professional at the beautiful Royal Jersey Golf Club in Grouville, Tommy is noted for the accuracy rather than the power of his shots and he has been a consistent tournament winner since he won his first event, the RTV International, back in 1968. One of his outstanding successes was in the 1970 South African Open against strong opposition that included the redoubtable Gary Player who had almost made the title his own personal property. In the same year he captured the PGA Match Play championship. Born in St Helen's, Lancashire, in 1941, Tommy was in Ernest Button's training scheme aimed at creating a world-challenging British golfer and he benefitted from the coaching of one of his heroes, Max Faulkner. He has made several spirited challenges for the Open championship and was seventh in 1970, equal fifth in 1976 and top-placed Briton in ninth place in 1977.

STARFILE No. 7

DAVID GRAHAM
My Six Favourite Golf Courses

1 **PEBBLE BEACH**, California
2 **AUGUSTA NATIONAL**, Georgia
3 **MERION GOLF CLUB**, Ardmore, Pennsylvania
4 **PINE VALLEY**, New Jersey
5 **PRESTON TRAIL**, Dallas, Texas
6 **ROYAL MELBOURNE**, Black Rock, Victoria

'Every golf course has its own special identity but for me personally these rate highest of all. They are all picturesque, beautifully manicured and present a challenge at every hole. I am especially fond of the Merion Golf Club because that is where I became the first Australian to win the U.S. Open in 1981. There are so many wonderful golf courses around the world that it would have been much easier to have made a list of fifty rather than six!'

MY BOYHOOD GOLFING HEROES: Kel Nagle, winner of the British Open in 1960, was my hero at home in Australia. The two overseas golfers whose performances I followed with most interest were Arnold Palmer and Gary Player and my admiration for their ability and their achievements is as strong as ever.

MY MOST MEMORABLE TOURNAMENT: My proudest achievement was becoming the first Australian to win the U.S. Open in 1981. The championship was staged at the Merion Golf Club and I shot 68−68−70 for the first three rounds to go into the final round three strokes behind leader George Burns. I managed to get everything together for the last eighteen holes and hit every green in regulation strokes and I only missed the fairway once from the tee. My final round score was 67 and I not only made up the three strokes on George Burns but finished three ahead of him, with Bill Rogers sharing the runners-up place. I stuck to my game plan throughout the tournament and felt mentally sharp and in total control of my swing, especially down the final stretch.

THE GREATEST CHAMPIONSHIP-WINNING PERFORM-ANCE: I'm sure that I am in good company when I select Tom Watson's victory in the 1977 British Open at Turnberry as the greatest championship-winning performance. Watson shot an incredible twelve-under-par total of 268, which chopped eight strokes off the Open record set by Arnold Palmer in 1962. It gave him victory by one stroke over Jack Nicklaus who had shot final rounds of 65 and 66 and still lost!

THE SPORTSMAN I MOST ADMIRE OUTSIDE GOLF: Bjorn Borg, and not only because of his great ability and the way he conducted himself on court. I admire the way he retired when he wanted to and while at the very top of his sport. That's a hard decision and it takes a special kind of man to make it.

FOR THE RECORD

DAVID GRAHAM, born in Windsor, Australia, in 1946, had set his sights on a career in golf from early childhood and he defied parental orders and left school on his fourteenth birthday to take a full-time job at the Riversdale Golf Club near Melbourne. He was a natural left-hander but the Riversdale professional George Naismith convinced him he would be better off playing orthodox right-handed golf. It has certainly proved the right way for David who, since moving to Florida and then Dallas, has established himself as one of the most respected shot-makers on the professional tour. He is noted for steady rather than spectacular play and also for his deadly accuracy. In his early days on the Tour he was a real have-clubs-will-travel professional and won tournaments in South Africa, Mexico, Thailand, New Zealand, Japan, South America, France and Britain. He won the Piccadilly Match Play championship in 1976 and established himself in the superstar bracket with victory in the 1979 U.S. PGA championship after a play-off with Ben Crenshaw. His round of 67 that clinched the U.S. Open title at Merion in 1981 was rated one of the finest rounds of championship golf ever played.

BOB CHARLES
The Three Greatest Left-Handed Golfers of My Lifetime

1 **RUSS COCHRANE** *(USA)*
2 **YAKUTA HAGAWA** *(Japan)*
3 **SAM ADAMS** *(USA)*

'I promise you it was not easy coming up with just these three names. I'm told that Australian Harry Williams was as good as any left-hander that ever stepped on to a tee but I never had the good fortune to see him play. Russ Cochrane revealed class and consistency on the U.S. Tour in 1983 when he won two tournaments. Yakuta Hagawa was the winner of the Japanese Open in 1981 and great things are expected of him. Sam Adams won the Quad Cities tournament some years ago but no longer plays the U.S. Tour.'

MY BOYHOOD GOLFING HEROES: The two golfers I went out of my way to read about were Sam Snead and Ben Hogan. They had a magical aura about them, Snead with his smooth-as-silk swing and Hogan with his unbelieveable determination. They were perhaps the two greatest golfers of all time. Need I say more?

MY MOST MEMORABLE TOURNAMENT: My victory in the British Open at Royal Lytham in 1963 stands out in my memory. I recorded rounds of 68−72−66−71 and averaged thirty putts a round. This was good enough to tie the 277 aggregate score of American Phil Rodgers, with Jack Nicklaus a stroke back in third place. Rodgers and I played off over thirty-six holes and in the morning round I got my putter working really well and needed only twenty-six putts on the way to a 69 and a three-shot lead at the halfway point. In the afternoon round I took thirty-one putts for a score of 71 to 76 by Rodgers. So I won by eight shots to become the first New Zealander and the first left-hander to win the Open or, for that matter, any of the major championships. It was a proud moment when I collected the coveted trophy.

THE GREATEST CHAMPIONSHIP-WINNING PERFORM-ANCE: The one I enjoyed above all others was Tony Jacklin's British Open victory at Royal Lytham in 1969. It was one of the few occasions I have played with a major championship winner on the final round and so I got the best possible view of every shot and was able to drink in the wonderful atmosphere along with Tony. Both Tony and I scored 72 for the last eighteen holes which left me two shots behind him in second place. It was a marvellous occasion.

THE SPORTSMAN I MOST ADMIRE OUTSIDE GOLF: Bjorn Borg, whose temperament was outstanding particularly under any sort of pressure. He competed with complete control of his emotions and his conduct was a great example to all young sportsmen.

FOR THE RECORD

BOB CHARLES is a natural right-hander who became a left-handed golfer by happy accident. When he first took up the game he borrowed his father's set of left-hand clubs and has been playing the 'wrong' way round ever since. In 1963 he beat American Phil Rodgers in a play-off for the Open championship at Royal Lytham to become the first New Zealander and the only left-hander ever to win a major golf title. Born in Carterton, New Zealand, in 1936, Bob is a cool, phlegmatic character who plays his golf without fuss but with a smoothness and style that sets him apart from the powerhouse players who have become prominent on the professional circuit. The most impressive feature of his game is his control and mastery around the green, particularly his putting which − during his peak years − was as close to perfect as you can get. One of his greatest performances came in the 1969 World Match Play at Wentworth when, with a procession of prodigious putts, he saw off first Maurice Bembrige, Tommy Aaron in the semi-final and then Gene Littler in the final. Littler was rated one of America's finest putters but he had to bow to the superiority of Charles who continually sank putts of more than twenty-five feet. He has won only one major championship but has twice finished third in the U.S. Open and was runner-up for the U.S. PGA title in 1968. As he approaches the veteran stage, Charles continues to grace the game with his seemingly effortless golf and remains a respected tournament player.

Bob Charles...for whom the left way has been the right way

Tony Jacklin...gave British golf its biggest boost

STARFILE No. 9

TONY JACKLIN
The Ten Greatest Golfers I Have Seen

1. **JACK NICKLAUS** *(USA)*
2. **BEN HOGAN** *(USA)*
3. **SEVE BALLESTEROS** *(Spain)*
4. **TOM WATSON** *(USA)*
5. **GARY PLAYER** *(South Africa)*
6. **SAM SNEAD** *(USA)*
7. **LEE TREVINO** *(USA)*
8. **ARNOLD PALMER** *(USA)*
9. **PETER THOMSON** *(Australia)*
10. **BOBBY LOCKE** *(South Africa)*

'Jack Nicklaus and Ben Hogan stand out on their own, with Seve Ballesteros catching up if he can capture a few more of the major championships. Of the old-timers, I suppose Bobby Jones would be up there competing for first place but it's impossible to make a judgement because I didn't have the good fortune to see him play. Another favourite of mine, who should perhaps be somewhere in the list, is Argentinian Roberto de Vicenzo who won nearly 250 tournaments in a long and distinguished career.'

MY BOYHOOD GOLFING HEROES: Ben Hogan because of his courage and character as well as his skill...Sam Snead because of his dream of a swing...and Arnold Palmer because he made golf such an exciting and entertaining spectacle.

MY MOST MEMORABLE TOURNAMENT: Two share equal place — the British Open of 1969 and the U.S. Open of 1970. In winning them I became the only British golfer to have held both the British and U.S. Open championships at the same time. The only players to have done it before me were Americans Bobby Jones, Gene Sarazen, Ben Hogan and Jack Nicklaus, so I was in the best possible company. From a nostalgic point of view, I suppose becoming the first British-born Open champion since Max Faulkner in 1951 has to take first place. But for sheer satisfaction, nothing could beat standing on the final tee in the U.S. Open at Chaska, Minnesota, with a six-stroke lead over the greatest golfers in the world. I will never forget holing a long final putt for a 70 and victory by seven shots in a championship that I led from start to finish. Neither will I ever forget the incredible scenes as I walked down the final fairway at Royal Lytham on my way to the British Open after I had hit a perfect drive off the final tee that virtually clinched my victory.

THE GREATEST CHAMPIONSHIP-WINNING PERFORM-ANCE: I have seen so many outstanding title-winning performances that I find it almost impossible to narrow it down to naming just one. But if you twist my arm I will plump for Johnny Miller's incredible last round 63 in the 1973 U.S. Open when he made up six strokes to win the championship. It was as near a perfect round as you can get.

THE SPORTSMEN I MOST ADMIRE OUTSIDE GOLF: Two stand shoulder to shoulder — tennis champions Rod Laver and Bjorn Borg. Both were great masters of their sport and gave everybody a perfect lesson in how a champion should handle himself in victory and defeat.

FOR THE RECORD

TONY JACKLIN gave British golf its biggest boost of all time when he won the 1969 British Open and the 1970 U.S. Open in the space of just eleven months. Cynics are quick to point out that he was unable to maintain this skyscraping standard but nobody can ever take away from him the fact that for a short spell in his career he was undoubtedly one of the world's great golfers. Born in Scunthorpe in 1944, Tony turned professional at seventeen in 1962 after representing England in boys internationals. He became assistant professional at the Potters Bar Club in Hertfordshire and in 1963 entered the British Open for the first time. He finished thirtieth at Royal Lytham, the same course on which he was to become a national hero six years later. His big breakthrough came when he won the Greater Jacksonville Open in Florida in 1968, the first major victory in America by a British-based golfer for forty-eight years. In the 1970 British Open at St Andrews he reached the turn in the first round in 29 but play was washed out by a storm and he finally finished the tournament as highest placed Briton in fifth position. He was third in 1971 and looked in a winning position in 1972 until Lee Trevino pulled off a series of magical shots to clinch his second successive Open victory. Now based at the magnificent Sotogrande golf course on the Costa del Sol, Tony is giving more and more concentration to television golf commentaries and he speaks with the same authority with which he plays the game.

STARFILE No. 10

BRIAN HUGGETT
The Six Greatest Welsh Wizards of My Lifetime

1 **DAI REES**
2 **IAN WOOSNAM**
3 **DAVE THOMAS**
4 **PHILIP PARKIN**
5 **CRAIG DeFOY**
6 **SID MOULAND**

'Dai Rees was not only the greatest of all Welsh golfers but also, in my opinion, the greatest British golfer not to win the Open. It certainly wasn't for the want of trying. He was fourth in 1946, third in 1950 and runner-up in 1953, 1954 and 1961. Dave Thomas, an incredibly long hitter, was born in Newcastle but was a regular in the Welsh World Cup squads.'

MY BOYHOOD GOLFING HEROES: Dai Rees (of course) and that battling Birmingham professional Charlie Ward, both of whom had a similar short build to me and so their success gave me encouragement. Another player I admired in my youth was the Irishman Harry Bradshaw, who was always so consistent and came so agonizingly close to winning the British Open in 1949.

MY MOST MEMORABLE TOURNAMENT: The Dunlop Masters at Royal Lytham in 1970. There was a strong, difficult wind blowing as I set off for the final round but I managed to master the conditions and equalled the course record with a 65. This gave me an aggregate total of 293 and victory over runner-up David Graham, with a young Peter Oosterhuis in third place.

THE GREATEST CHAMPIONSHIP-WINNING PERFORM-ANCE: Possibly because it's still fresh in the mind but I go for the 1984 British Open victory at St Andrews of the brilliant Spaniard Seve Ballesteros. Seve had to show great character and nerve to win following a dreadful year in the United States. His performance proved to the Americans that he was the world's best player, just when he needed to and in the world's greatest championship.

THE SPORTSMAN I MOST ADMIRE OUTSIDE GOLF: I admired Scottish international footballer Denis Law for his great flair and devilment. There has rarely been a player to match him for goal-mouth reactions. I liked the way he ended his career with something invested wisely in an era when they didn't get paid the fortunes that can be made in today's football.

FOR THE RECORD

BRIAN HUGGETT was fittingly dubbed 'The Toy Bulldog' because of his determined spirit and great strength of character that shone through in many tough tournaments. He developed a superb technique to overcome his handicap of being short and stocky and he became a golfer in the class of his countryman Dai Rees. For Brian, there can be no higher praise. He twice finished in the top three in the British Open: third behind Arnold Palmer and Kel Nagle in 1962, and joint second with Christy O'Connor behind champion Peter Thomson in 1965. Born in Porthcawl in 1936, he joined the tournament circuit in 1961 and for the next two decades was one of Britain's most consistently successful golfers. He won the German, Dutch and Portuguese Open championships and defeated John Panton in the 1968 PGA Match Play final. A resolute competitor in six Ryder Cup teams, he was seen in tears by millions of television viewers after he had holed a long putt to halve his match against Billy Casper in 1969. He thought the putt had clinched a Ryder Cup victory for Great Britain but the match finally ended in a tie. Brian briefly became club professional at the exclusive St Pierre Golf and Country Club follwing his retirement from the tournament tour in 1980 but then switched to organizing business golf events.

STARFILE No. 11

CRAIG STADLER
Three Tigers Who Can Roar Off the Tee

1 **GREG NORMAN** *(Australia)*
2 **JACK NICKLAUS** *(USA)*
3 **LANNY WADKINS** *(USA)*

'These are the three greatest drivers that I have come up against during my pro career. Each of them continually hits the ball long and straight with their driver and the three of them can find that vital extra twenty yards when it is most needed.'

MY BOYHOOD GOLFING HEROES: Arnold Palmer was the player whose game most appealed to me. I liked his 'go for it' attitude and the way he always generated excitement when he was on a charge followed by his vast army of fans.

MY MOST MEMORABLE TOURNAMENT: My victory in the 1982 Masters at Augusta is etched into my memory for all time. I opened with a 75 in unusually poor weather conditions that wrecked a lot of cards. Then a 69 second round and a 67 in the third put me into a three-stroke lead. Everything went smoothly for the first eleven holes of the final round and I was six strokes ahead of the field with seven holes to play. Then I had the nightmare of bogeying three of the last four holes and I couldn't help remembering how the same thing had hapened to Ed Sneed in the 1979 Masters when I had been playing with him. My collapse meant that Dan Pohl, with a final round of 67, was able to force a tie on 284 and we went into a sudden-death play-off. At the first hole of the play-off − the tenth − I got down in a par-four for victory and my first major championship. You could say it had been quite an experience!

THE GREATEST CHAMPIONSHIP-WINNING PERFORM-ANCE: It has to be the 'shoot out' between Tom Watson and Jack Nicklaus for the British Open at Turnberry in 1977. I doubt if there has ever been anything quite like their final two rounds when they were playing together and matching each other stroke for stroke. It's almost unbelievable that Jack shot a 65 and a 66 yet lost by a stroke.

36

THE SPORTSMAN I MOST ADMIRE OUTSIDE GOLF: I have eyes only for golf and so there is no one particular sportsman that I admire above others. I just like the guys who get on with their job and play their sport to win. It's the same in all sports, to get to the top and stay there you've got to 'go for it'.

FOR THE RECORD

CRAIG STADLER, affectionately known on the golf circuit as 'The Walrus', is a powerful striker of the ball and can also play the short game with precision, particularly on the green where he is famous for sinking pressure putts. Born in San Diego in 1953, he showed immense promise in his teens and won the World Junior championship in 1971. Two years later he was U.S. Amateur champion and was an impressive member of the U.S. Walker Cup team at St Andrews in 1975. The highlight of his professional career to date was a victory in the 1982 U.S. Masters when he won at the first hole of a sudden-death play-off after threatening to run away with the title. British golf followers remember him for his scorching first round 64 in the Open at Royal Birkdale in 1983. He led for the first two rounds but could not maintain his form as he had in the Kemper Open in Maryland in 1981 when he put together a remarkable sequence of 67−69−66−68 for a record ten under par total of 270. Craig has disciplined himself to bring a hot temper under control and on his day is as accomplished a golfer as there is on the professional circuit.

STARFILE No. 12

BRIAN BARNES
The Best of British

1 MAX FAULKNER
2 TONY JACKLIN
3 HENRY COTTON
4 BERNARD GALLACHER
5 TOMMY HORTON
6 NICK FALDO
7 SANDY LYLE
8 DAI REES
9 SAM TORRANCE
10 CHRISTY O'CONNOR Snr

'Max Faulkner was a master of all the golfing arts. He could almost make the ball sit up and talk with his irons. Max has had a tremendous influence on my career and I hold him in the highest esteem. For me, he is the Number One.'

MY BOYHOOD GOLFING HEROES: At home, it was Max Faulkner. He brought colour, flair and personality to golf. My favourite overseas player was the one and only Arnold Palmer, who was at his brilliant peak when I was playing in my first youth championship matches.

MY MOST MEMORABLE TOURNAMENT: The Tournament Players' championship at Dalmahoy in 1981. I had been in the dumps for most the of the year and it didn't look as if things would change when I went into the final round of the championship six strokes behind leader Brian Waites. I then produced a round of 62, which is the third lowest in European Tour history. Everything went to perfection over the last nine holes and I came home in 28, which included a two at the 309-yard seventeenth when I finished just a foot from the flag with my drive. I made up the six strokes on Waites and we went into a sudden-death play-off which I won at the fourth extra hole.

THE GREATEST CHAMPIONSHIP-WINNING PERFORM-ANCE: The head-to-head between Tom Watson and Jack Nicklaus in the 1977 Open at Turnberry is my choice. Both men played magnificent golf throughout the tournament with nothing to choose between them. There were three winners at Turnberry. Tom Watson took the championship and Jack Nicklaus won friends and admirers with his determination and stunning play. The third winner was the game of golf.

THE SPORTSMAN I MOST ADMIRE OUTSIDE GOLF: World snooker champion Steve Davis whose concentration and killer instinct would be well suited to the professional golf tour.

FOR THE RECORD

BRIAN BARNES, as you might have guessed from reading this Starfile, has been greatly inspired by 1951 British Open champion Max Faulkner, who is not only his coach but also his father-in-law. Born in Addington, England, of Scottish parents in 1945, Brian has carried some of his mentor's famous eccentricity into his golf and it is nothing unusual to see him playing in colourful Bermuda shorts or with a pipe clenched between his teeth. There are few players in the world who can match him for power and, when in the right mood, this beefy giant of a man can beat just about anybody. Proof of this came in the 1975 Ryder Cup when twice in one day he emerged a winner against the great Jack Nicklaus. He travels well and he has been Open champion of Holland, France, Spain, Italy, Portugal, Zambia and Kenya, and he was Australian Masters champion in 1970. A keen fisherman, Brian has been one of the enigmas of British golf. He has always had the potential to be up there with the kings of the game but has never quite got it together in the major championships by which greatness is measured.

STARFILE No. 13

PETER ALLISS
The Greatest Golfers I Have Seen

1 **ARNOLD PALMER** *(USA)*
2 **JACK NICKLAUS** *(USA)*
3 **BOBBY LOCKE** *(South Africa)*
4 **PETER THOMSON** *(Australia)*
5 **BEN HOGAN** *(USA)*
6 **SAM SNEAD** *(USA)*
7 **HENRY COTTON** *(Great Britain)*
8 **TOM WATSON** *(USA)*
9 **SEVE BALLESTEROS** *(Spain)*
10 **LEE TREVINO** *(USA)*

'I must stress that these are not listed in any particular order. The word "great" is much overused and abused in sport but it is a description that fits each and everyone of the ten players listed here. All of them have been "great" golfers in their own way and it has been my pleasure and privilege to have seen them play.'

MY BOYHOOD GOLFING HEROES: Dick Burton, winner of the Open in 1939 and sadly unable to benefit greatly from it because of the war; also Jimmy Wade and — naturally — my father, Percy Alliss, of whom Henry Cotton once said: 'He has one of the neatest swings I have ever seen.'

MY MOST MEMORABLE TOURNAMENT: The Esso Round Robin Match Play tournament at Moor Park in 1964. My record was: played fourteen, won twelve, drawn one, lost one. I had amassed sufficient points to have the event won with a full round still to go. It was a super feeling knowing I had wrapped it all up with some of the best golf I had ever played in my life. That was the highlight of the year in which I won the Harry Vardon Trophy for the first time for leading the Order of Merit.

THE GREATEST CHAMPIONSHIP-WINNING PERFORM-ANCE: The 1977 Open at Turnberry. Both Tom Watson and Jack Nicklaus set a scoring record of 203 for the first fifty-four holes. Watson, with a total of 200, created new figures for the last fifty-four holes including a final round of 65 which was the best ever by a champion. But what made this Open so spectacular was the long, old-fashioned duel between the greatest player of modern times and the man destined to succeed him. It's doubtful whether this two-man duel will ever be beaten for drama and excitement.

THE SPORTSMAN I MOST ADMIRE OUTSIDE GOLF: Jockey Lester Piggott, a superpro whose dedication and desire has made him one of the Great Untouchables of sport. And just to think, he's never allowed himself the reward of a decent meal!

FOR THE RECORD

PETER ALLISS has taken over from his close friend, the late, legendary Henry Longhurst, as the 'Voice of Golf'. His commentaries on BBC TV and in the United States are steeped in the authority that satisfies the experts; yet they are at the same time lightly laced with the sort of humour and anecdote that gives the golf an appeal to those who perhaps think of a caddie as something in which to keep the tea. Peter was born into golf. He arrived at the first tee of life in 1931 in Berlin where his father, Percy, was a club professional. Percy had a superb swing that Peter inherited and he was widely recognized as one of the finest strikers of a golf ball in the world. If he had been as efficient on the greens as he was on the fairways there is little doubt that he would have been a major force on the world circuit. He won twenty premier tournaments in Europe between 1954 and 1969 including the Italian, Spanish and Portuguese Opens in three successive weeks in 1958. Since retiring from international golf in 1969, this suave, debonair character has become a household name as a television personality and he continues to have an influence on the golf world as a respected course architect and prolific author of golf books. He talks an even better game than he played. And that's saying something.

Peter Alliss...the 'Voice of Golf'

Lanny Wadkins...a bold, attacking player

STARFILE No. 14

LANNY WADKINS
The Six Greatest Short-Game Players

1 **TOM WATSON** *(USA)*
2 **TOM KITE** *(USA)*
3 **SEVE BALLESTEROS** *(Spain)*
4 **BEN CRENSHAW** *(USA)*
5 **ISAO AOKI** *(Japan)*
6 **GARY PLAYER** *(South Africa)*

'All are modern-era players whose records speak for themselves. Their accuracy around the greens with the short irons means they are always in with chances of birdies and eagles. It's an education to watch them at work. They are real masters of the art of chipping, pitching and putting.'

MY BOYHOOD GOLFING HERO: Sam Snead was the golfer I took a shine to, just like every other youngster where I grew up. I was born and raised in Virginia, the state where Slammin' Sam was king and so I just naturally favoured him. I couldn't have had a better player to look up to and from whom to draw inspiration.

MY MOST MEMORABLE TOURNAMENT: The U.S. PGA championship at Pebble Beach, California, in 1977. I'd suffered through quite a dry spell due mainly to illness and my victory in the PGA was a tremendous boost for my confidence. Gene Littler looked destined to win when he held a five-shot lead with nine holes to play. I kept in striking distance thanks to two eagles on the front nine and I drew closer as Gene dropped shots on five of the first six holes on the back nine. Jack Nicklaus started one of his charges and led at the fifteenth but he bogeyed the par-three seventeenth while I had a birdie at the par-five eighteenth to tie with Littler on 282. For the first time a major championship was to be decided by a sudden-death play-off and I had to sink a twenty-foot putt to stay in the championship at the first hole. I finally clinched the championship with a four to Gene's five on the third hole. The victory worked wonders for me and two weeks later I shot a record 267 to win the World Series.

THE GREATEST CHAMPIONSHIP-WINNING PERFORM-ANCE: I've seen nothing to match Ray Floyd's performance in the 1976 Masters at Augusta. He led from start to finish and his 271 gave him an eight-stroke victory over Ben Crenshaw. He had twenty-one birdies and an eagle and it looked as if he was going to hole every shot he hit. Ray shot 65–66–70–70 and didn't allow anybody a chance to get anywhere near him.

THE SPORTSMAN I MOST ADMIRE OUTSIDE GOLF: Mickey Mantle, a legendary baseball star with the New York Yankees, is the sportsman I've always admired. He hit 536 home runs before crippling injuries that handicapped him for much of his career forced his retirement. He was a brilliant outfielder and could hammer the ball out of the park both right-handed and left-handed.

FOR THE RECORD

LANNY WADKINS was an outstanding amateur golfer and made an immediate impact on the professional circuit after winning the U.S. Amateur championship in 1970. He was Rookie of the Year in 1972 and quickly became one of the leading money winners. Ill health and major surgery anchored Lanny's progress in the mid-1970s but he proved he has fighting qualities to go with his talent by battling back into the front rank of world golfers after a nightmare couple of years during which he was dogged by bad luck. He had a memorable battle with the esteemed veteran Gene Littler in the 1977 U.S. PGA championship at Pebble Beach, California, coming from behind to force a sudden-death play-off which he won at the third hole. Born in Sam Snead country at Richmond, Virginia, in 1949, Lanny has some of 'Slammin' Sam's' flair and style and is one of the most respected players on the tough, highly competitive American Tour. Always exciting to watch because of his bold, attacking tactics, he can take any course apart when at his best. He proved this with a 69–66–67–65 sequence to win the 1977 World Series at Akron and he recorded 65–70–63–65 to win the Phoenix Open in 1982. His younger brother, Bobby, is also a first-rate golfer.

STARFILE No. 15

MICHAEL BONALLACK
My Identikit of the 'Perfect' Golfer

The **DRIVING POWER** and **ACCURACY** of **JACK NICKLAUS**
The **LONG IRON SHOTS** of **SAM SNEAD**
The **SHORT GAME** of **SEVE BALLESTEROS**
The **BUNKER SHOTS** of **GARY PLAYER**
The **PUTTING** of **TOM WATSON**
The **TEMPERAMENT** of **LEE TREVINO**

'My vote for the "perfect" player would have gone to Ben Hogan had he possessed the short-game artistry of Seve Ballesteros. However, as he did not, I have to favour Jack Nicklaus as the nearest there has been to a "perfect" golfer.'

MY BOYHOOD GOLFING HEROES: Henry Cotton and Bobby Jones, two names that I was brought up with. In my childhood there was no television and these two golfers had more written about them than any other players. More photographs of their swings and analysis of their technique was available and I used to read everything I possibly could about them.

MY MOST MEMORABLE TOURNAMENT: Great Britain's victory over the United States in the Walker Cup at St Andrews in 1971. It was only the second time we had won the Cup (1938 was the first) and I had long cherished the ambition to be in a winning team. To be captain was an added bonus. The match had particular significance because it was the fiftieth anniversary of the first informal match in 1921. We set up the victory by winning six of the final afternoon's singles. They were all close encounters, two of the victories coming on the seventeenth green and four on the last green.

THE GREATEST CHAMPIONSHIP-WINNING PERFORM-ANCE: Tom Watson's one-stroke victory over Jack Nicklaus in the 1977 Open at Turnberry ranks as the greatest of all championship contests. An over-imaginative scriptwriter could not have come up with anything quite as thrilling as an Open in which the world's two greatest players have three identical rounds of 68−70−65 and then play together in the final round, one scoring 65 and the other

66. It is the stuff of which fantasties are made, yet it really happened and Watson had the Open championship trophy to prove it, while Nicklaus must have wondered how on earth he had lost after scoring an aggregate 269. It was quite unbelievable.

THE SPORTSMAN I MOST ADMIRE OUTSIDE GOLF: West Indies cricketer Sir Gary Sobers, for his pure natural ability as a batsman, bowler and fielder. He enjoyed every minute of cricket and life and conveyed this feeling to everybody lucky enough to see him in action.

FOR THE RECORD

MICHAEL BONALLACK, now the distinguished secretary of the Royal and Ancient, was quite simply the finest post-war British amateur golfer ever to grace the game; perhaps the finest of all time. He was a Walker Cup player without break from 1959 to 1973 and played in a record twenty-five matches. Born in Chigwell, Essex, in 1934, and educated at Haileybury School, Michael was as equally accomplished at cricket as at golf but chose to concentrate on the small-ball game after winning the 1952 Boys' championship. He was considered by many good judges to have had the best short game of any British golfer, amateur or professional. His long list of title victories included the Amateur championship in 1961–65–68–69–70 and the English Amateur Stroke Play in 1964–68–69 (tied)–71. He was the leading amateur in the Open championship twice, in 1968 and 1971. President of the English Golf Union in 1982, he took over the prestigious post of Secretary of the Royal and Ancient the following year.

STARFILE No. 16

BERNARD HUNT
The Ten Greatest British Golfers of My Lifetime

1. HENRY COTTON
2. DAI REES
3. CHRISTY O'CONNOR Snr
4. NEIL COLES
5. ERIC BROWN
6. PETER OOSTERHUIS
7. NICK FALDO
8. PETER ALLISS
9. TONY JACKLIN
10. HARRY WEETMAN

'These are listed as they came to my mind rather than in any order of merit. Henry Cotton made a big impression on me because he won his third Open at Muirfield in 1948 just after I had started making my living at the game. He set high standards for all British golfers to follow and showed what could be achieved with the right application and dedication.'

MY BOYHOOD GOLFING HEROES: Two American golfing giants, Sam Snead and Ben Hogan, claimed my undivided attention when I was a youngster. Sam Snead...for his wonderful swing and rhythm which never seemed to alter, and also for his sense of humour and amusing throw-away comments; Ben Hogan...for his book, *Modern Fundamentals*, which became my bible. Alas, I never quite mastered it.

MY MOST MEMORABLE TOURNAMENT: The Dunlop Masters at Portmarnock in 1965. I finished the last round in 65 to beat Peter Thomson who had held a comfortable lead going into the last day. I won with an aggregate 283, one more than when I had finished first in the Dunlop Masters at Little Aston two years earlier.

THE GREATEST CHAMPIONSHIP-WINNING PERFORM-ANCE: Gary Player's Open championship victory at Carnoustie in 1968. He didn't strike the ball at all well in the first two rounds but kept his hopes alive with precise pitching, putting and sheer hard graft. As the week went on he got better and better and thoroughly deserved his hard-earned victory. He finally won with a 289, with Jack Nicklaus and Bob Charles a stroke behind in joint second place.

THE SPORTS STAR I MOST ADMIRE OUTSIDE GOLF: Virginia Wade always had my support and sympathy. I think she probably suffered badly from nerves yet still managed to become champion in the centenary year at Wimbleon. It was a marvellous achievement because it is always so much harder to win in front of a home crowd. The pressure is that much greater.

FOR THE RECORD

BERNARD HUNT was one of the greatest British golfers never to win the Open. He was third in the 1960 championship and finished in the top five on four occasions. His class and consistency is reflected in the fact that he won the Harry Vardon Trophy for the lowest stroke average in 1958, 1960 and 1965. He could burn up any course when at his brilliant best as he revealed at Wentworth in 1966 in the Picadilly Stroke Play tournament. Bernard recorded rounds of 66–63–66–67 and his fifty-four-hole total of 195 equalled the second lowest of all time. He unveiled his vast potential when on his way to victory in the 1953 Spalding tournament, going out in 28 for the first nine which remains the second lowest nine-hole score in championship history. In his 'golden year' of 1963, he won four major British events with aggregates of 272, 273, 282 and 270. He collected fifty-five under-fours and thirty-nine birdies and what was then record prize money for the season of £7209. Born into a golf-steeped family at Atherstone in 1930, Bernard and his younger brother Geoffrey both won Ryder Cup places. Geoffrey took over from his father as club professional at Hartsbourne, while Bernard is based as resident professional at Foxhills in Ottershaw, Surrey, where he has built a reputation as a highly respected teacher.

STARFILE No. 17

BERNARD GALLACHER
My Six Favourite Golf Courses

1 ROYAL BIRKDALE
2 ST ANDREWS
3 MUIRFIELD
4 WENTWORTH
5 SUNNINGDALE
6 BERKSHIRE

'Each of these courses has been designed utilizing the natural environment, keeping artificial construction to an absolute minimum. I have not listed them in any particular order although Royal Birkdale is, for me, the best of all the courses.'

MY BOYHOOD GOLFING HEROES: There were six who had a special place in my affections – Gary Player, Arnold Palmer, Tony Lema, Peter Alliss, David Thomas and Eric Brown. Inevitably, Jack Nicklaus took over in later years. I was winning my first Boy International honours with Scotland when Jack was starting to establish himself as the world's Number One.

MY MOST MEMORABLE TOURNAMENT: The most memorable moment of my career was beating one of my boyhood heroes, Gary Player, for the Dunlop Masters title at St Pierre in 1974. Gary and I tied for first place with an aggregate total of 282 and I managed to beat him in the sudden-death play-off. I retained the Dunlop Masters title at Ganton the following year, the first time the tournament had been won by the same player in consecutive years.

THE GREATEST CHAMPIONSHIP-WINNING PERFORMANCE: I rate the 1984 Open victory by Seve Ballesteros the best performance I've seen in a major championship. He played some magnificent golf to hold off Tom Watson and his final long putt on the seventy-second hole was a fitting way to clinch the title.

THE SPORTSMAN I MOST ADMIRE OUTSIDE GOLF: Bobby Charlton, the Manchester United and England footballer, was the sportsman I always admired. He represented his sport with dignity and style on and off the pitch and was always the complete professional.

FOR THE RECORD

BERNARD GALLACHER, born at Bathgate in 1949, has been one of Britain's leading golfers since joining the professional circuit in 1968 after winning the Scottish Open Amateur Stroke Play championship. He revealed enormous potential while still a schoolboy and was a Boys' International representative in 1965 and 1966. In only his second year on the European Tour he won the coveted Harry Vardon trophy for the lowest stroke average and, at twenty, was the youngest recipient of the award. Apart fom his two triumphs in the Dunlop Masters, he has won four Scottish Professional championships, the Spanish, French and Zambian Open titles and he was the Tournament Players champion in 1980. He is a single-minded competitor whose finest golf has been produced for Britain in Ryder Cup combat. The highlight of his Ryder Cup career was a four and three victory over Lee Trevino on the final day of a tied match in 1969. He showed remarkable consistency throughout 1969. His successes included victories in the Wills and Schweppes tournaments and he was voted Scottish Sportsman of the Year. His putting is particularly effective as he proved in the 1971 Martini International at Norwich. He looked out of the hunt after an opening round of 80 but then got to work with his putter to record 67−68−67 for a dramatic victory. Bernard, beaten by Bobby Wadkins in a sudden-death play-off for the European Open championship in 1978, has the plum job of professional at Wentworth.

STARFILE No. 18

KEN BROWN
The Six Greatest Short-Game Players

1 **SEVE BALLESTEROS** *(Spain)*
2 **TOM WATSON** *(USA)*
3 **ISAO AOKI** *(Japan)*
4 **GARY PLAYER** *(South Africa)*
5 **HUBERT GREEN** *(USA)*
6 **MANUEL PINERO** *(Spain)*

'These are the six most accomplished short-game players that I have seen. All are masters on or near the green and are always in with a shout for birdies because of their accuracy and skill. Seve in particular is a genius with the short irons and produces tournament-winning shots from impossible positions.'

MY BOYHOOD GOLFING HEROES: The two whose fortunes I followed with closest interest were Lee Trevino and Gary Player. Both are flair players and have shown an astonishing consistency in the major tournaments. Their performances when I was a teenager helped stimulate my interest in the game.

MY MOST MEMORABLE TOURNAMENT: The British Open at Muirfield in 1980. I was in contention going into the final day after rounds of 70, 68 and 68. The third round was particularly memorable because I was paired with one of my boyhood heroes, Lee Trevino, and I managed to make up a three-shot deficit and draw level with him in second place behind Tom Watson. My final round of 76 was a disappointment but I had the satisfaction of matching Watson's two at the seventh.

THE GREATEST CHAMPIONSHIP-WINNING PERFORM-ANCE: I have not seen a championship-winning performance to top that of Seve Ballesteros when he captured the British Open at St Andrews in 1984. His battle over the last eighteen holes with Tom Watson was a classic, and the way he drilled in his final putt from fifteen feet to clinch the championship was pure magic.

THE SPORTSMAN I MOST ADMIRE OUTSIDE GOLF: Jockey Lester Piggott, for his single-mindedness and great resilience. His all-time record of twenty-eight Classic victories over a span of more than thirty-five years speaks volumes, not only for his great riding ability but also for his self-motivation and iron discipline. It's incredible the way he just keeps going.

FOR THE RECORD

KEN BROWN is an Anglo-Scot who was born in Harpenden, Herts on 9 January 1957. He turned professional in 1975 after winning the prestigious Boys' International the previous year. Ken was the constant companion of controversy early in his career because of the slow pace of his play and his apparent disregard of authority. But no amount of criticism could disguise the fact that he is an immensely gifted golfer who has benefited from coaching by 'The Maestro' Henry Cotton. Pencil-slim and gangling, he is deceptively powerful, and his short game is a thing of perfection over which he refuses to be hurried. He has improved his image in recent years and experience on the tough U.S. Tour has made him a more complete golfer. Ken has the same sort of single-minded approach to his sport that he admires so much in master jockey, Lester Piggott. Increased confidence and maturity have brought a new composure and control to his game and it seems only a matter of time before he captures one of the major championships. He has total belief in his own ability which puts him ahead of most players at the first tee.

STARFILE No. 19

MAURICE BEMBRIDGE
My Identikit of the 'Perfect' Golfer

The **DRIVING POWER** and **ACCURACY** of **JACK NICKLAUS**
The **LONG IRON SHOTS** of **ARNOLD PALMER**
The **SHORT GAME** of **SEVE BALLESTEROS**
The **BUNKER SHOTS** of **GARY PLAYER**
The **PUTTING** of **TOM WATSON**
The **TEMPERAMENT** of **BOB CHARLES**

'The player who, in my opinion, has come closest to being "perfect" is the great Ben Hogan. I've gone for the temperament of Bob Charles because he never allows anything to interrupt his concentration on a golf course. I remember his coolness in the 1963 Open at Royal Lytham after Phil Rodgers had holed first in the play-off and then covered the hole with his hat in a display of showmanship. The delay made no difference to the phlegmatic Charles and he sunk his putt and went on to win. I have selected the short game of Seve Ballesteros because he is the only man alive who could posibly get up and down from the ballwasher!'

MY BOYHOOD GOLFING HEROES: Ben Hogan, who was perfection personified; Arnold Palmer, who played the game as no other before him and revolutionized golf by introducing the power approach; David Snell, my tutor, who gave me the best possible foundation for my game.

MY MOST MEMORABLE TOURNAMENT: The tournament that will always remain in my memory is the 1974 U.S. Masters when I produced a final round of 64 to equal the course record set by the one and only Jack Nicklaus. My inward half of 30 also equalled the course record. I finished ninth overall in a championship won by Gary Player.

THE GREATEST CHAMPIONSHIP-WINNING PERFORM-ANCE: My nomination has to be Arnold Palmer's first British Open victory at Royal Birkdale in 1961. He conquered the course and the vicious winds with some phenomenal iron play and bold putting. This was Palmer at his peak, and he proved that with his long irons he was second to none. The weather was absolutely atrocious, particularly on the second day when the the wind roared so hard it blew marquees down. Palmer started his round when the wind was at its strongest, yet managed to birdie five of the first six holes by rifling iron shots under the wind with a power and accuracy that was quite extraordinary.

THE SPORTSMAN I MOST ADMIRE OUTSIDE GOLF: Dr – now Sir – Roger Bannister, who set new standards in athletics when he became the first man to break the four-minute mile barrier in 1954. He always represented his sport with great dignity and never once did he degrade it through 'shamateurism'.

FOR THE RECORD

MAURICE BEMBRIDGE, born at Worksop on 21 February 1945, has become a have-clubs-will-travel globetrotting professional since marrying his pretty American wife, Suzie, and is a frequent competitor on the Far East, Australasia and United States circuits. He has been three times winner of the Kenyan Open, captured the German Open in 1975 and was runner-up in the New Zealand Open in 1971 and again the following year. His 63 in the qualifying round for the 1967 British Open equalled the championship record, and he also equalled the U.S. Masters record with a 64 in the final round at Augusta, Georgia, in 1974. He hit a barren spell in the late 1970s but scorched back to winning form with an impressive victory in the Benson and Hedges International in 1979. His best overall performance in the British Open came in 1968 when he was the highest-placed home-based golfer in fifth place, four shots behind champion Gary Player.

STARFILE No. 20

NICK FALDO
My Identikit of the 'Perfect' Golfer

The **DRIVING POWER** and **ACCURACY** of **JACK NICKLAUS**
The **LONG IRON SHOTS** of **TOM WEISKOPF**
The **SHORT GAME** of **SEVE BALLESTEROS**
The **BUNKER SHOTS** of **SEVE BALLESTEROS**
The **PUTTING** of **TOM WATSON**
The **TEMPERAMENT** of **JACK NICKLAUS**

'There is no such thing as the "perfect" golfer, but you would be close to finding him if you could put these skills into one player. Jack Nicklaus has come near to being perfect but is let down by a poor short game. Tom Weiskopf has a dream of a swing and all the right attributes but he lacks real desire. If he had Nicklaus's competitive attitude and temperament he would be one of the untouchables. A player with the long game of Jack Nicklaus, the short game of Seve Ballesteros and the putting of Tom Watson would be quite a golfer!'

MY BOYHOOD GOLFING HEROES: I didn't have one in particular but admired all the 'greats' — old-time giants like Bobby Jones, Sam Snead and Henry Cotton and modern masters such as Arnold Palmer, Gary Player, Lee Trevino and, of course, Jack Nicklaus.

MY MOST MEMORABLE TOURNAMENT: My proudest moment came in 1977 when, at 20, I became the youngest golfer ever to play in the Ryder Cup. I partnered Peter Oosterhuis to beat Ray Floyd and Lou Graham on the first day and then we beat Jack Nicklaus and Ray Floyd on the second day. To cap it all I had a one-hole victory over Tom Watson on the final day. My most satisfying moment since then was winning the 1984 Heritage Classic, my first victory on the U.S. Tour.

THE GREATEST CHAMPIONSHIP-WINNING PERFORM-ANCE: The 1984 British Open victory of Seve Ballesteros at St Andrews stands out above all the others I've seen. Seve had gone into the championship on a slump after nearly a year of not having won a title and following a miserable time on the U.S. Tour. But he showed tremendous character and produced his best golf when it really mattered. He curbed his natural aggression and played a beautifully controlled game despite the pressure put on him by Tom Watson, who was going all-out for a record-equalling sixth British Open victory. I managed to finish top British challenger for the third successive year but ruined my chances with a third round 76 and was six shots adrift of Seve at the end.

THE SPORTSMAN I MOST ADMIRE OUTSIDE GOLF: Bjorn Borg, for his great composure and skill and setting an example as to how a great champion should conduct himself. I would also like to give a mention for a sports *woman* I admire — Michelle Moulton, an outstanding driver in a very gruelling sport dominated by men.

FOR THE RECORD

NICK FALDO, born at Welwyn Garden City on 18 July 1957, was an exceptional prospect from his early teens and turned professional in 1976 after winning the English Youth and then the English Amateur championship. His sensational debut in the 1977 Ryder Cup came in a season when he was out on his own as 'Rookie of the Year', and he has since produced a procession of outstanding performances that have firmly established him as one of Britain's finest post-war golfers. His peak year to date was 1983 when he became the first player to win more than £100,000 on the European Tour and the first player since Bernard Hunt (1963) to win five 72-hole tournaments in a season; he was also the first English professional to top the European order of merit since Peter Oosterhuis in 1974. He gained new confidence when capturing the 1984 Heritage Classic on the U.S. Tour and many fine golf judges think it only matter of time before he wins the British Open title that he wants above all others.

SECTION TWO
THE IMMORTALS

THE REDOUBTABLE BOBBY JONES

1 Robert Tyre Jones, born in Atlanta, Georgia, on 17 March 1902, was arguably the greatest golfer of all time and certainly the greatest amateur player. In a span of just eight years from 1923 he won thirteen of the world's major titles – the U.S. Amateur five times, the U.S. Open four times, the British Open three times and the British Amateur championship once.

2 Jones was just nine when he won the Junior championship at his club, East Lake, and fourteen when he captured his first Georgia state title. In 1917 he was the Southern Amateur champion and the following year made his debut in the U.S. Open, finishing in a tie for eighth place. He was runner-up in both the Canadian Open and U.S. Amateur championship in 1919.

3 In his first challenge for the British Open at St Andrews in 1921 he finished an angry and frustrated second to the course. He took 46 to the turn in the third round, then started the homeward journey with two sixes and finally tore up his card at the short eleventh. He later learned to control his brittle temper and also to love St Andrews, of which he said in 1958: 'If I were allowed only one course in the world on which to play golf I would choose St Andrews.'

4 It was 1923 when Jones established himself as the world's greatest golfer. He beat Bobby Cruickshank in a play-off for the U.S. Open and over the next seven years never failed to win at least one major championship. Jones turned down numerous offers to switch to the professional circuit, preferring to concentrate on his studies. He held degrees in engineering, science and law and started a law practice in Atlanta after leaving Harvard.

5 Jones represented the United States in six Walker Cup matches including two as captain and was undefeated in singles play. He won three of the four British Open championships in which he competed and in his last nine U.S. Opens was champion four times and runner-up four times. From 1923 to 1930 he lost only once in match play over thirty-six holes, going down to George von Elm in the U.S. Amateur final of 1926 when bidding for a third successive championship.

58

6 In his early days on the golf circuit he based his style of play on that of Scots-born Stewart Maiden, the professional at his local East Lake Club. He later developed his own smooth, rhythmic swing that featured a hip turn through ninety degrees. The strain of maintaining his form under the constant attention of huge galleries and the media took its toll on Jones who had a nervous, highly strung temperament. He often used to lose a stone in weight during major championships and suffered strength-sapping bouts of sickness.

7 He achieved a unique Grand Slam in 1930 – the British Open, the British Amateur, the U.S. Open and the U.S. Amateur. Jones completed what became known as 'The Impregnable Quadrilateral' in the U.S. Amateur at Merion, beating Eugene Homans on the eleventh green in the final for an eight and seven victory. There was such intense interest in his progress that just one American newspaper sent sixteen writers and photographers to cover his every move, and he had to have a bodyguard of fifty U.S. Marines to protect him from the thousands of spectators thronging the course.

8 The strain was all too much for Jones and the 1930 U.S. Amateur was his last championship. He retired from competitive golf at the age of twenty-eight to concentrate on his law practice. He kept in touch with the game as an esteemed writer and also with a series of instructional films; and he designed the first matched set of flanged irons for Spalding that were in demand around the world.

9 Jones continued to play at his beloved Augusta National course, which was built to his design, but without the competitive drive of his peak years. He remained the motivating power behind the famous Masters tournament right up until his death in 1971 at the age of sixty-nine.

10 He began to suffer from a muscular disease in the 1950s and was eventually confined to a wheelchair. There was a moving ceremony at St Andrews in 1958 when he was made a freeman of the old burgh. Bobby Jones will always be a freeman of golf, the game he graced with great skill and sportsmanship.

THE INCREDIBLE WALTER HAGEN

1 Walter Hagen, born at Rochester, New York, on 21 December 1892, won the British Open four times, the United States Open twice, and five U.S. PGA championships. Four of his PGA Match Play triumphs came in consecutive years from 1924 to 1927 and during one stunning sequence he won twenty-two individual matches in succession.

2 Hagen was a colourful, flamboyant character whose approach to life was summed up by his famous quote: 'Be sure to smell the flowers along the way.' 'The Haig' changed the cloth-cap image of the professional golfer by leading a champagne-style life, always arriving at the course in a chauffeur-driven limousine and staying at the best hotels. He used to keep his eye in at London's Savoy Hotel by driving the ball from the hotel roof into the Thames.

3 The son of an $18-a-week blacksmith of German descent, Hagen first got the urge to play golf while caddying at 10 cents an hour at his local Rochester club. He became an assistant professional at the club and his natural flair for the game was quickly obvious. He made his competitive debut in the Canadian Open in 1912. Asked how he had got on by his club members back at Rochester, he said: 'I lost.' It was a remark that summed up his approach to golf. He was interested only in being a winner.

4 He won his first U.S. Open in 1914 and evidence of his staying power is that he finished third in the same tournament twenty-one years later. Hagen could raise his game to a pitch where he was just about unbeatable as in winning the Western Open in 1916 when he played five consecutive holes in just thirteen strokes.

5 A master of head-to-head match play, his most satisfying victory came in 1926 when he beat the great Bobby Jones (usually his master in tournament play) by the astonishing margin of eleven and ten in a seventy-two-hole challenge match. Two years later he himself lost a seventy-two-hole challenge match to Britain's Archie Compston by eighteen and seventeen, but he got quick revenge the following week when he won the British Open championship.

6 He became the first American-born winner of the British Open in 1922 and was the first American to capture both the British and U.S. Open championships. Another famous first came in 1927 when he captained the winning United States team in the first ever Ryder Cup match at Worcester, Massachusetts. He played in all the Ryder Cup matches until 1937.

7 Hagen, a master showman who almost glowed with self confidence, played on more than 2,500 courses during his twenty-five-year career and earned more than one million dollars. He raised the standards and earnings potential for all professionals and Gene Sarazen said: 'All those of us who have got the chance of making big money in golf should say a silent prayer of thanks to "The Haig". He made it all possible.'

8 During the 1929 Open at Muirfield, Hagen was spotted playing cards in the lounge of the Marine Hotel. It was three o'clock in the morning, just hours before the final round. One of his supporters, hoping to convince him to retire, told him that his closest rival Leo Diegel had been in bed for hours. 'I'm sure he has,' said Hagen, barely looking up from his card hand. 'But is he sleeping?' Later that day he clinched his fourth Open victory.

9 In 1919 in the U.S. Open at Brae Burn, Hagen needed a birdie three on the last hole to win over Mike Brae who was the leader in the clubhouse with 301. The Haig fired his second shot to the heart of the green and then summoned Brae out to watch him take his eight-foot putt which stopped just half an inch short of the hole. The next day he won the eighteen-hole play-off after telling Brae: 'Roll your sleeves up, Mike, so that the gallery can see your muscles quivering.'

10 He loved to put pressure on opponents with his gamesmanship that was never allowed to spill over into bad sportsmanship. Often when in a bunker, he would send his caddie forward to the green to remove the flag. It was not all an act because he was one of the finest short-game players there has ever been. The Haig died in Traverse City, Michigan, in 1969 but his name will always live on in golfing legend.

THE GREAT GENE SARAZEN

1 Born in Harrison, New York, on 27 February 1902, of Italian parents, Gene Sarazen (original name, Eugene Saraceni) learned his golf as a caddie in Apawamis. When he won the U.S. Masters at his first attempt in 1935 he became the first man to capture what has become known as the 'Big Four' — the U.S. and British Opens, the U.S. PGA and the U.S. Masters.

2 Sarazen started playing golf in a bid for fitness after an attack of pleurisy. He found he had a natural aptitude for the game and became a caddie and golf club assistant. Aged just twenty, he made a sensational start to his professional career when he won the U.S. Open at Skokie, Illinois, with a title-clinching final round of 68. In that same year — 1922 — he won the U.S. PGA but it was a victory that was devalued because Walter Hagen was not competing.

3 He and Hagen became close friends but intense rivals on the golf course. After his U.S. Open-PGA double triumph of 1922, Sarazen challenged 'The Haig' to a seventy-two-hole match for what was billed as a world-championship decider. Sarazen won and repeated his victory in the U.S. PGA final the following year, a see-sawing match that was not decided until the thirty-eighth hole.

4 Visiting Britain for the first time in 1923, he had a nightmare in the Open at Troon, failing to qualify because of a wind-ruined round of 85. He vowed he would return to win even if he had to swim. In 1928 he finished second and he was third in 1931. His determination was rewarded in 1932 when he won the Open at Sandwich with a total of 283, which was to be the lowest for eighteen years.

5 Standing just 5 feet 5 inches tall, he never allowed his lack of inches to handicap him. He was a powerful striker of the ball and a master of the short game, particularly with the sand wedge that he invented and with which he could perform miraculous shots. Following the meteoric start to his career he ran into problems with his technique but once he had cured a wayward hook he re-established himself as a golfing master.

6 Sarazen ended his major championship drought in dramatic style in 1932. Leaning heavily on the local knowledge of caddie Skip Daniels, he won the British Open at Prince's, Sandwich, with a record aggregate of 283 and victory by five strokes from his countryman Macdonald Smith. The following month he won the

U.S. Open, coming from behind to take the title thanks to a record final round of 66. He completed the last twenty-eight holes in just one hundred strokes.

7 Defending the British Open championship at St Andrews in 1933 he finished just one shot off a three-way tie with Densmore Shute and Craig Wood and he also missed the chance of a major championship by just one shot in the 1934 U.S. Open at Merion.

8 He had a remarkable victory in the U.S. Masters in 1935. Craig Wood looked a certain winner until Sarazen holed a full-blooded wooden second shot for an albatross at the fifteenth. He finished tied with clubhouse leader Wood and won the play-off by five strokes.

9 Sarazen, who lost only one singles in six consecutive appearances in the Ryder Cup between 1927 and 1937, made a bold bid to win the U.S. Open title in 1940, eighteen years after his first victory. He finished runner-up after forcing a play-off with Lawson Little. A colourful figure in his trademark plus-fours, he has remained a familiar figure in world golf throughout the post-war years and he and Byron Nelson launch the U.S. Masters each year with a ritual nine-hole match.

10 At the age of seventy-one, this popular character made a sentimental journey back to Royal Troon and was in the headlines during the 1973 Open. He struck a magnificent five-iron at the 'Postage Stamp' eighth on the first day and holed-in-one. On the second day at the same hole, he played out of a bunker and holed his second shot. So he had found the hole twice in successive days without need of his putter and had wiped out the memory of his nightmare British debut at Troon fifty years earlier.

THE MAESTRO HENRY COTTON

1 Henry Cotton, born in Holmes Chapel, Cheshire, on 26 January 1907, was Britain's outstanding golfer over a span of two decades. He won three British Open championships and would undoubtedly have collected more but for the interruption of the Second World War when he was at his peak. Throughout his competitive career he was supported and encouraged by his Argentinian-born wife Toots, an accomplished golfer in her own right and a continual source of inspiration.

2 Acknowledged by his contemporaries as one of the greatest strikers of a ball there has ever been, Cotton was arguably the best of all British golfers and without question the most dedicated. He spent so many hours practising that he often couldn't stand up straight because of back cramps and he developed a permanent list because he spent so much time locked in his right-shoulder-down golf stance.

3 All his practice led to him developing immense strength in his hands and they became a focal point of his simple, uncomplicated three-quarter swing. He had such control of all his clubs that he could almost make the ball sit up and talk. Even his rivals called him 'The Maestro' and he was a showman who perfected a stage act that was good enough to get him a top-of-the-bill spot at London's Coliseum where he entertained the audience with trick shots and passed on playing tips.

4 Educated at public school in Dulwich, Cotton was so keen to master the game of golf that he travelled to the United States at the age of twenty-one to play and to study techniques. He was greatly influenced by the master teacher Tommy Armour and he proved his trip had paid off the following year when in his first Ryder Cup match he beat highly rated American Al Watrous by four and two.

5 He was assistant professional at Fulwell, Rye, at seventeen and two years later was appointed professional to Langley Park Club. After winning four successive Kent Open titles, he widened his experience with trips abroad during which he won the Mar del Plata Open in Argentina and the Belgian Open, and after finishing first in the 1932 PGA Match Play championship in 1933 he became the resident professional at the Waterloo Club in Belgium.

6 In 1934 at Sandwich he ended ten years of American domination of the British Open with a stunning exhibition of golf that touched perfection. He opened with rounds of 66 and a record 65 and after a third round of 72 he was twelve strokes ahead

of his nearest rival. Stomach cramps severely handicapped him in the final round and his magical touch deserted him. He struggled round in 79 but it was still good enough to give him victory by five shots in a record-equalling aggregate of 283.

7 Three years later at Carnoustie Cotton regained the Open championship against a strong field that included the entire United States Ryder Cup team. His last round of 71 in driving rain and on a waterlogged course was considered one of the finest ever played in an Open championship. He finished on 290, two ahead of Reg Whitcombe who retained the title for Britain the following year.

8 Cotton won fifteen championships in his frequent trips to the continent and played in the Ryder Cup matches of 1929, 1937 and 1947 when he was also captain. In 1953 he was appointed non-playing captain of Britain's Ryder Cup team. Invalided out of the RAF because of a poor constitution, he was awarded the MBE for his fund-raising services for the Red Cross.

9 Between 1930 and 1948 he was only once outside the top ten players in the Open. To build himself up for his 1948 challenge he went to the United States where better food was available to help restore him to the best of health. He was back to his brilliant best for the Open at Muirfield and a scorching second round 66 helped lift him to victory by five strokes. George VI was among his large gallery and 'King Henry' fittingly produced feats of golf fit to put before a king.

10 He continued to make appearances in the Open and was sixth in 1956 at the age of forty-nine and eighth two years later, but by then he was concentrating more on teaching and writing about the game to which he had given such distinguished service. He became director of the Penina Golf Hotel in Portugal and in recent years has passed on knowledgeable tips as a member of the BBC TV commentary team at the Open championship with which his name will always be linked.

THE POETIC BYRON NELSON

1 Byron Nelson, born at Fort Worth, Texas, on 4 February 1912, revolutionized golf with a new-style swing that was imitated by millions of players worldwide. Starting out like Ben Hogan as a caddie at the Fort Worth Club, he became the most copied of all golfers after he had dominated the U.S. Tour with five major championship victories and an unparalleled sequence of success.

2 Nelson turned professional in 1933, and just four years later won his first major championship in dramatic fashion. He picked up six strokes on leader Ralph Guldahl in just two holes in the final round of the 1937 U.S. Masters and went on to clinch the title with what was then a record 66. He scored a two and a three at the twelfth and thirteenth to a five and a six by Guldahl who finished runner-up two strokes behind Nelson's aggregate 283. There's a bridge and a plaque to commemorate this performance on the Masters course at Augusta, Georgia.

3 In 1939, Nelson established himself as the Number One player in the United States by winning the U.S. Open after a three-way play-off with Craig Wood and Densmore Shute, and adding to his championship collection the Western, North and Southern Opens as well as finishing runner-up in the U.S. PGA tournament (a title he won the following year).

4 He was exempted from military service during the Second World War because of haemophilia and he dominated the weakened American tournaments, adding a second U.S. Masters title in 1942 after he and his fellow-Texan Ben Hogan had forced a first-ever eighteen-hole play-off. Nelson gained five shots on Hogan in a stretch of eleven holes even though Hogan himself played them in one under par.

5 Nelson was never out of the money in an astonishing run of 111 successive tournaments yet was rarely full-time on the circuit, preferring to spend much of each season supplementing his income by teaching as a club professional. It was not until 1945 that he spent a full year on the PGA Tour and that was the season he rewrote the record books with a run of victories that made him a golfing immortal.

6 In 1945, aged thirty-three, Nelson won eleven consecutive U.S. PGA Open titles and finished first in nineteen of the thirty tournaments that he entered. He came second in eleven of the other competitions and averaged only 68.33 strokes per round. In

the nine stroke-play tournaments that he won, his average margin of victory was 6.3 strokes. The peak moment of his unforgettable year came when, competing in his fifth U.S. PGA championship final in five years, he won the title with a crushing four and three victory over Sam Byrd.

7 Cynics have since suggested it was made easier for him because many of his leading rivals were still on military service. Even if this were true, his scoring was phenomenal and has never been matched for consistency. The fact is that most of the top golfers *did* compete against him and his rivals on the 1945 Tour included players of the calibre of Ben Hogan, Sam Snead, Jimmy Demaret, Mike Turnesa and Densmore Shute.

8 It was after his stunning successes of 1945 that golfers, amateur and professional, started to copy Nelson's upright, one-piece, flex-kneed swing in which the left side was dominant and featured a full shoulder turn and a very straight left arm.

9 Nelson won the first two tournaments of the following season and then announced his retirement from the professional tour. He had been plagued by a nervous stomach because of his non-stop search for perfection and he felt physically drained. He settled down with his wife on the Texas ranch he had always dreamed of owning.

10 He made occasional appearances in selected tournaments, winning the Bing Crosby Invitational in 1951 and the French Open in 1955. His influence on golf carried on through his instructional books and he became one of the most renowned teachers of the game whose constructive thoughts were often heard on television in America where he was a regular commentator. Bobby Jones paid him the greatest of all compliments when he said in 1945: 'At my best, I never came close to the golf Nelson shoots.' He and Gene Sarazen make an annual pilgrimage to Augusta to play the opening nine-hole match at the U.S. Masters.

Byron Nelson...led a swinging revolution

Sam Snead...whose swing is the sweetest thing

THE SWINGIN', SLAMMIN' SAM SNEAD

1 Sam Snead, born in Hot Springs, Virginia, on 27 May, 1912, turned professional in 1934 and over the following forty years registered more than 160 victories, including eighty-four official U.S. PGA tournament titles. Nobody has been able to match his longevity in championship-class golf and he recorded top ten finishes in the U.S. Open, Masters and PGA while in his mid-fifties, and in 1971 – aged sixty-seven – he became the first player ever to beat his age in an official PGA event.

2 The fifth son of a cow-and-chicken farmer, he first learned golf by watching his oldest brother, Homer, smacking shots across the back pasture of their small farm. He carved his own clubs out of swamp trees and started to copy his brother, learning accuracy at an early age because there were so few balls available that he had to know where every one landed. Snead became first a caddie and then a professional at his local Greenbrier course at Sulphur Springs.

3 He won his first major Tour event in 1937 – the Oakland Open – and that same year made his Ryder Cup debut. He lost only one of six Ryder Cup singles (a one-hole defeat by Harry Weetman at Wentworth in 1953) and he was non-playing captain of the U.S. team that tied with Great Britain in 1969.

4 Snead, reckoned to have the sweetest swing in golf, won seven major championships – three U.S. Masters, three U.S. PGA championships and the British Open. His victory in the Open came at St Andrews in 1946 when, despite an indifferent last round of 75, he still had four shots to spare over joint runners-up Johnny Bulla and Bobby Locke.

5 The one title that always eluded him was the U.S. Open. He was runner-up in 1937, 1947, 1949 and 1953. When he came to the final tee in 1937 he thought he needed a par-five to win and, after hitting his drive into trouble, tried a series of prodigious recovery shots and finished taking an uncharacteristic eight. He later discovered that a six would have been sufficient to have taken the title.

6 He recorded the first sub-60 round in an American tournament with a 59 on his home course of White Sulphur Springs in 1959. He completed the last nine holes in 28, with a birdie three at the last hole. Snead followed this with a second round of 63 for an all-time record aggregate for thirty-six holes of 122. Fittingly, the tournament in which he was competing was called the Sam Snead Festival.

7 Elected U.S. PGA Player of the Year in 1949, he celebrated over the following twelve months by winning ten tournaments. His triumphs in this golden year included two majors — the U.S. Masters and the U.S. PGA. It was his second of three Masters victories, finishing with two 67s for an aggregate of 282. His total for the last two rounds was a fourteen-stroke improvement on his first two rounds played in gale-force winds.

8 His third Masters success came in 1954 when he beat his great rival Ben Hogan 70—71 in a play-off after they had overtaken virtually unknown amateur Billy Joe Patton in the last three holes after Patton had looked like causing one of the shock upsets of the century. Snead came close to a fourth Masters title in 1957. He led by three strokes going into the final round but was overhauled by Doug Ford who holed out from the bunker at the eighteenth for a championship-clinching 66.

9 In 1965 he became — at fifty-two — the oldest player to win a major tournament when he captured the Greater Greensboro Open. He won five world senior professional titles — 1964, 1965, 1970, 1972 and 1973 — and continued to lure thousands of spectators who wanted a view of the smoothest and most famous swing in golf.

10 Snead, who holed-out-in-one on twenty-four occasions, finished third equal in the 1974 U.S. PGA championship that he had first won thirty-two years earlier. He was sixty-two years old. Earlier in the season he had finished second in the Los Angeles Open with a six-under-par aggregate on the challenging Riviera Country Club course. For long-playing standards alone he deserves his Golf Hall of Fame place, and the fact that he played the game with such style and finesse simply added to the legend of Slammin' Sam Snead.

THE UNBELIEVABLE BEN HOGAN

1 Ben Hogan, born in Dublin, Texas, on 13 August 1912, achieved golfing immortality between 1946 and 1953 by winning the U.S. Open four times, the Masters twice, the American PGA twice and the British Open at his first and only attempt. His life story was featured in the first full-length film ever made about a professional golfer, *Follow the Sun*, in which he was portrayed by Glenn Ford.

2 The film was made in 1951 and spotlighted Hogan's remarkable come-back to golf after a 1949 car crash in which he received serious injuries that threatened to end his playing career. Incredibly, he produced his greatest golf *after* the accident – and after the film.

3 Hogan started taking a close interest in golf from the age of eleven when – like Byron Nelson – he used to caddie at Fort Worth. He turned professional at eighteen but struggled to establish himself and he was twenty-seven before he won his first tournament. He spent as many as ten hours a day practising until he had perfected his swing and in 1946 all the hard work started to pay off when he won his first major title, the U.S. PGA championship at Portland. He started the final eighteen holes three shots down to Ed 'Porky' Oliver but reached the halfway stage in just thirty shots and was then two strokes up, a lead he never relinquished.

4 His feat of winning in the one golden year of 1953 the Masters and the U.S. and British Opens was a unique hat-trick. He entered only five tournaments that year – and won them all. He achieved his Masters victory with a record aggregate of 274, including three successive rounds of 69, 66 and 69 for a five-stroke victory over runner-up, his old rival Porky Oliver.

5 He completed the second leg of his triple Grand Slam in the U.S. Open at Oakmont. Hogan led the competition from start to finish and his four-round aggregate of 283 gave him a six-stroke victory over Sam Snead who had to be content with second place in the event for a fourth time. It was Hogan's fourth U.S. Open title, equalling the record set by Willie Anderson and Bobby Jones.

6 Hogan was criticized for never having entered the British Open and it was whispered that he was frightened of British conditions.

He silenced his critics by going to Carnoustie, beating the course record and winning the Open by four strokes to complete his hat-trick. Hogan got better and better at Carnoustie as he settled into his smooth rhythm. He opened with a 73, followed it with a 71 and a 70 before really taming the course with a brilliant final round of 68.

7 He won sixty-two tournaments on the U.S. Tour and would have won many more but for putting that was sometimes loose and unpredictable. From tee to green, there has rarely, if ever, been anybody to touch him for sheer accuracy. He more than any other golfer proved that practice makes perfect.

8 One of his few disappointments was failing to win the U.S. Open for a fifth time. He surprisingly lost to unheralded Jack Fleck in a play-off for the coveted championship at the Olympic Club, San Francisco in 1955. The following year he finished just a stroke behind Cary Middlecoff after missing a short putt that would have forced a play-off.

9 He continued to play on through middle-age and as late as 1967 — at the age of fifty-four — shot a record-equalling 30 on the back nine in the Masters for a third-round 66.

10 Hogan was voted America's 'Sportsman of the Decade, 1946–56', and in 1965 U.S. golf writers named him the greatest professional golfer of all time. A dour, serious-minded, unemotional man who gave every ounce of concentration to his golf, Hogan was once asked to recall his greatest shot. 'I only remember the bad ones,' he replied, which summed up his totally committed approach to the game. Little wonder that the spectators at Carnoustie in 1953 nicknamed him 'The Wee Ice Mon'. If they had made a sequel to the biopic film *Follow the Sun* they would have had to call it *Superman* because in golfing terms that's exactly what he was.

THE BRILLIANT BOBBY LOCKE

1 The son of a Belfastman, he was born Arthur D'Arcy Locke at Germiston, Transvaal, on 20 November 1917, but became known on the golf courses of the world as 'Bobby'. The Americans paid him the compliment of calling him 'the Bobby Jones of South Africa'. His achievements included four British Open titles and fourteen victories on the tough United States circuit.

2 Locke turned professional after winning his second South African Amateur championship in 1937. He was five times South African Open champion before joining the South African Air Force in 1940 and during the next five years flew more than one hundred Liberator missions.

3 He won three more South African Open titles after the war and in 1947 took on and beat the best of the Americans on the United States Tour during which he was affectionately dubbed 'Old Muffin Face'. He finished first in four out of five consecutive tournaments and won seven in all. Sam Snead accepted the challenge of a sixteen-match 'head to head' series in South Africa and was beaten twelve—two with two matches squared. He was Locke's equal from green to tee but was out-classed on the greens where the South African had no master.

4 His style was hardly conventional. He hit every wood and long-iron shot way out to the right with a deliberate hook but the ball always came back on course. His contemporaries consider him the greatest putter there has ever been. He religiously went through the same routine on the green for every putt, whether it was from twenty feet or twenty inches. It was a careful, perfectionist's technique that was copied by professionals the world over.

5 He won the British Open four times, in 1949, 1950, 1952 and 1957. Irishman Harry Bradshaw looked bound to win at Sandwich in 1949 but his ball lodged in the mouth of a broken bottle and he took a six after playing it as it lay. He finished level with Locke on 283 and the South African won the thirty-six-hole play-off by twelve shots.

6 There was a controversial climax to his 1957 Open victory at St Andrews. Locke had a four-shot cushion on the rest of the field as he hit his second shot to the heart of the green. He marked his ball two-putter-lengths off the line so that his playing partner could putt out. When he replaced his ball he inadvertently put it back only one putter's length away. The length of the putt was unaltered

but the line was and there was a complaint made that he had infringed the rules. The Championship Committee sensibly decided that he had gained no advantage and, as he had won by three shots, ruled that the result should stand, which pleased every fair-thinking golf follower.

7 Evidence of Locke's worldwide success is that he won Open championships in New Zealand, Canada, France (twice), Germany, Switzerland and Egypt. He won fourteen tournaments in the United States and was twice third in the U.S. Open.

8 Competing in the Chicago Victory National championship in 1948, he defeated his nearest rival in a top-class field by an astonishing sixteen strokes which remains the largest winning margin in U.S. Tour history. In two bids for the U.S. Open he finished third in 1947 and fourth in 1948.

9 A familiar figure in his plus-fours, white cap and tie, Locke was sometimes criticized for his slow, calculating play but nobody could deny the success of his methods. He was a master of pitching as well as putting and he holed-out-in-one fifteen times. A fourteen-handicapper at the age of eight, Locke played with the same hickory-shafted putter from the age of eighteen until his final tournament. No putter has given better service to its master.

10 His competitive career was finished by injuries received in a car smash in 1968 but he was back at St Andrews in 1976 along with Walter Hagen and Henry Cotton to receive honorary membership of the Royal and Ancient Club.

THE AMAZING ARNOLD PALMER

1 Arnold Palmer, born in Latrobe, Pennsylvania, on 10 September 1929, did more than anybody to transform golf into a booming world sport played and followed by millions. He captured the public imagination with his dashing, adventurous approach to the game during a fifteen-year span as the dominant personality on the world golf stage. At his peak, he won eight major championships, earned more than two million dollars and became one of the best known and popular of all sportsmen.

2 His incredible popularity was reflected by the size of the galleries that followed him around the world's golf courses. His supporters became collectively known as 'Arnie's Army' and even today as he approaches the veteran stage he is still assured of a massive following every time he sets foot on to a fairway in any sort of tournament and revives memories of when the Palmer 'charge' became one of the most exciting sights in sport.

3 The son of a professional at the Latrobe Country Club, Palmer was an exceptional player from his early teens and turned professional after winning the American Amateur championship in 1954. Within a year of joining the Tour he had captured his first premier title, scorching to the Canadian Open title in 1955 with rounds of 64−67−64−70 for his best-ever aggregate total of 265.

4 Palmer won nine tournaments in his first three years as a professional but had to wait until 1958 before capturing his first major championship − the U.S. Masters. He shot birdies on the final two holes to win by a stroke from joint runners-up Doug Ford and Fred Hawkins and to become, at twenty-eight, the youngest Masters champion since Byron Nelson in 1937.

5 In 1960 he regained the Masters and then added the U.S. Open, a victory that helped lay the foundation to the legend that is Arnold Palmer. He went into the final round six strokes behind leader Mike Souchak, proceeded to birdie six of the first seven holes and reached the halfway mark in a record-equalling thirty strokes. He finished with a 65 and victory by two strokes over a young amateur answering to the name of Jack Nicklaus.

6 Palmer went to St Andrews in the summer of 1960 to try to emulate Ben Hogan by winning the British Open at his first attempt and complete the Masters−U.S. Open−British Open hat-trick. He made a great tilt at the title with a 70−71−70−68 sequence but was pipped by one stroke by Australian Kel Nagle.

But Palmer's charisma had caught the public imagination on both sides of the Atlantic and, helped by Mark McCormack's inspired management, he became a household name even in houses where people didn't know the difference between an eagle and an albatross.

7 He breathed new fire and interest into the British Open and returned to Birkdale in 1961, this time overcoming gale-swept conditions to win the championship with adventurous, attacking golf that thrilled his growing army of fans. He rated the golf he produced in the first six holes of the second round — three under par in appalling weather — the best he had ever played and a wondrous shot to the fifteenth green out of an impossible lie is commemorated with a plaque.

8 Palmer pulverized the field to retain the Open at Troon in 1962, winning by six strokes from runner-up Kel Nagle and setting an aggregate record of 276. In the same year he won the ·U.S. Masters for a third time and was beaten in a play-off for the U.S. Open by the young pretender to his throne, Jack Nicklaus.

9 The one title that was always out of his reach was the U.S. PGA championship in which he was three times the runner-up, the last time in 1970 when Dave Stockton produced a third round 66 on his way to a two-stroke victory. Palmer's last major victory before a hip problem led to a power cut was in 1964 when he shot 60−68−69−70 for a memorable fourth triumph in the Masters at Augusta.

10 He was voted American Athlete of the Decade in 1970, and even into the 1980s he produces occasional flashes of his old genius for the game that made him a hero of heroes for golfers and spectators alike. In all he won sixty-one premier tournaments but, more than that, he brought the magic of golf to the masses.

JACK NICKLAUS, KING OF CLUBS

Jack Nicklaus has been a winner all his golfing life. He has won more major titles — nineteen — than any other golfer in history and he is the only player to have won each of the five major championships: British Open, U.S. Open, U.S. Masters, U.S. PGA and U.S. Amateur. As well as his victories, he has had eight seconds and two thirds in the U.S. Open, seven seconds in the British Open, four seconds in the U.S. Masters and four seconds in the U.S. PGA. He has scored more than ninety victories since turning professional in 1962. These have been his major triumphs:

1959: U.S. Amateur; Royal St George's Challenge Cup
1960: Eisenhower Trophy (Team and Individual)
1961: U.S. Amateur
1962: U.S. Open, World Series
1963: U.S. Masters, U.S. PGA, World Cup (Team and Individual), World Series
1964: Australian Open, World Cup (Team and Individual)
1965: U.S. Masters
1966: British Open, U.S. Masters, World Cup (Team)
1967: U.S. Open, World Cup (Team), World Series
1968: Australian Open
1970: British Open, Piccadilly Match Play, World Series
1971: U.S. PGA, Australian Open, Dunlop International, World Cup (Team and Individual)
1972: U.S. Open, U.S. Masters
1973: U.S. PGA, World Cup (Team)
1975: U.S. Masters, U.S. PGA, Australian Open
1976: Australian Open, World Series
1978: British Open, Australian Open
1980: U.S. Open, U.S. PGA

Nicklaus, born at Columbus, Ohio, on 21 January 1940, has been U.S. PGA Player of the Year five times (1967–72–73–75–76) and was leading money-winner eight times between 1964 and 1976 while on his way to accumulating a record haul of more than four million dollars. He was voted U.S. Sportsman of the Year in 1978, the Athlete of the Decade at the end of the 1970s and he was honoured with the Bobby Jones Award in 1975 and the Walter Hagen Award in 1980 for his services to golf.

CHAMPIONS OF CHAMPIONS

Ten golfers have won seven or more major championships during their careers:

19–JACK NICKLAUS *(USA)*
U.S. Open, 1962–67–72–80
British Open, 1966–70–78
U.S. Masters, 1963–65–66–72–75
U.S. PGA, 1963–71–73–75–80
U.S. Amateur, 1959–61

13–BOBBY JONES *(USA)*
U.S. Open, 1923–26–29–30
British Open, 1926–27–30
U.S. Amateur, 1924–25–27–28–30
British Amateur, 1930

11–WALTER HAGEN *(USA)*
U.S. Open, 1914–19
British Open, 1922–24–28–29
U.S. PGA, 1921–24–25–26–27

9–BEN HOGAN *(USA)*
U.S. Open, 1948–50–51–53
British Open, 1953
U.S. Masters, 1951–53
U.S. PGA, 1946–48

9–GARY PLAYER *(South Africa)*
U.S. Open, 1965
British Open, 1959–68–74
U.S. Masters, 1961–74–78
U.S. PGA, 1962–72

8–ARNOLD PALMER *(USA)*
U.S. Open, 1960
British Open, 1961–62
U.S. Masters, 1958–60–62–64
U.S. Amateur, 1954

8–TOM WATSON *(USA)*
U.S. Open, 1982
British Open,
 1975–77–80–82–83
U.S. Masters, 1977–81

7–HARRY VARDON
 (Great Britain)
British Open,
 1896–98–99–03–11–14
U.S. Open, 1900

7–GENE SARAZEN *(USA)*
U.S. Open, 1922–32
British Open, 1932
U.S. Masters, 1935
U.S. PGA, 1922–23–33

7–SAM SNEAD *(USA)*
British Open, 1946
U.S. Masters, 1949–52–54
U.S. PGA, 1942–49–51

SECTION THREEE
THE WINNING WOMEN OF GOLF

Many women have scorched the fairways and lit up the greens with their golfing exploits since the first ladies' golf club was formed at St Andrews in 1867. These have been among the leading lights of women's golf:

LADY MARGARET SCOTT won the first three British Ladies' championship finals, 1893-95. She beat Isette Pearson in the first two finals, seven and five in 1893 and three and two the following year. Her brother, the Hon. Michael Scott, won the British Amateur in 1933 at the age of fifty-five, the oldest man ever to win the trophy. Two other brothers, Osmund and Denys, contested the final of the Italian Amateur championship.

MAY HEZLET was just seventeen when she won both the Irish and British women's championships in 1899. She won three British titles, beating her sister Florence in the 1907 final. Another sister, Violet, was runner-up in 1911 and her brother, Charles, played in three Walker Cup matches.

CHARLOTTE (LOTTIE) DOD, born 24 September 1871, was the youngest Wimbledon champion of all time. She was fifteen years and 285 days old when she won the first of her five championships in 1887. She then switched with distinction to golf and won the British championship in 1904 by beating May Hezlet by one hole at Troon.

JOYCE WETHERED was eighteen when she entered the 1920 English Ladies' championship 'just for fun'. She was a shock winner, beating the experienced Cecilia Leitch by two and one in the final after trailing six down with sixteen to play. Joyce then started to take her golf seriously and retained the title over the next four years. She also won the Ladies' Open four times and shared in eight victories in the Worplesdon mixed foursomes with seven different partners. Joyce, who retired in 1937 after her marriage to Lord Heathcoat-Amery, was rated by her contemporaries as the supreme woman golfer.

CECILIA (CECIL) LEITCH, born in Silloth on the Solway Firth in 1891, was second only to the peerless Joyce Wethered as a major force in British golf between the two world wars. She won the British championship a record four times, was five times French champion and also held the English and Canadian titles. A powerful, attacking player, she lost three out of four British championship finals to Joyce Wethered. Their 1925 final at Troon, which Joyce won at the thirty-seventh, was considered one of the greatest classics in the history of women's golf.

GLENNA COLLETT, later Mrs Edwin Vare, captured the U.S. Ladies' championship a record six times between 1922 and 1935 but could never make the same impact in the British Ladies' championship. She was twice runner-up, once to Joyce Wethered and then to Diana Fishwick. Born in New Haven, Connecticut, in 1903, she was a massive hitter of the ball and at the age of just eighteen was able regularly to hit her drives to distances of up to 300 yards. She was known as 'the Bobby Jones of women's golf' and was a magnificent competitor in the Curtis Cup, playing each year from 1932 to 1948.

VIRGINIA VAN WIE, born in Chicago in 1909, had to live in the shadow of her great rival Glenna Collett for many years but had her fair share of successes including three consecutive victories in the U.S. Amateur championship. The sweetest of these was in 1932 when she conquered Glenna Collett ten and eight to make amends for crushing defeats of thirteen and twelve and six and five in previous finals. She retired after completing her championship hat-trick in 1934.

PAM BARTON, born in London in 1917, was – at seventeen – the youngest player ever to represent Britain in the Curtis Cup after winning the French Open in 1934. Two years later she won both the British Open championship and the American Women's Amateur championship, the first time this had been achieved since Scots-born Dorothy Campbell's double triumph in 1909. She was British Open champion again in 1939. A stocky, freckle-faced red-head from Royal Mid-Surrey, she was an exceptionally good short-game player and her death in a wartime flying accident while serving in the Women's Auxiliary Air Force was a major blow for British golf.

BABE ZAHARIAS was voted the greatest woman athlete of the half century in an Associated Press Poll in 1950. Born Mildred Didrikson of Norwegian parents in Texas in 1914, her legendary feats included gold medals in the 1932 Los Angeles Olympics in the javelin and eighty-metre hurdles, two selections in the All-American basketball team, three home runs in one game of baseball and success at diving, lacrosse and billiards! In 1934 she switched her attention to golf and over the next twenty years she provided plenty of evidence to suggest she was the greatest woman golfer of all time. Married to Greek wrestler George Zaharias, she toured the world giving exhibitions and winning tournaments galore. She won seventeen consecutive tournaments in 1947 including the British Ladies' championship, and she captured the World championship four times between 1948 and 1951. Few men could match her driving power. Her third U.S. Open triumph in 1954 followed an operation for cancer that finally claimed her life two years later.

PATTY BERG, born in Minneapolis, Minnesota in 1918, won more than eighty top tournaments during her twenty-year career and earned what was then a record $190,000 in prize money. An extrovert character with a bubbling personality, she teamed up with 'Babe' Zaharias to form a popular travelling golf clinic. At her peak she maintained a stroke average of around 74. She continued to compete at top level after recovering from a cancer scare in 1971 and still concentrates on her famous golf clinics that have done so much to help raise the all-round standard of women's golf in the United States.

LOUISE SUGGS, born in Atlanta, Georgia in 1923, won fifty tournaments on the U.S. Tour between 1949 and 1962 and was the first woman elected to the LPGA Hall of Fame. She won the U.S. Open championship in her first season in 1949, beating the great Babe Zaharias by fourteen strokes on her way to a then record aggregate of 291. She lowered the record to 284 when retaining the title in 1952 and was runner-up in the premier tournament four times.

VICOMTESSE DE SAINT SAUVEUR was one of Europe's leading women golfers for a span of nearly thirty years from 1937 when, as Mme Lally Vagliano, she won the British Girls' championship at Stoke Poges. She represented France in international events every year for a spell of twenty-eight years, broken only by the Second World War. The winner of every major European championship, she regained the Swiss Open title in 1965 — sixteen years after her first triumph. Her outstanding performance came in the 1950 British Ladies' championship final when she beat Jessie Valentine by three and two.

MARY (MICKEY) WRIGHT, born in San Diego, California in 1935, was four times winner of the U.S. Women's Open between 1958 and 1964 and was considered one of the longest hitters of the ball in the history of women's golf. She had a golden year in 1961 when she won ten tournaments, including four in succession. She included a 'faultless' round of 69 on her way to victory in the U.S. Open that year. Two years later she finished first in thirteen tournaments. Her eighty-two official tournament victories were a record until overtaken by Kathy Whitworth, and another record was her round of 62 at Midland, Texas, in 1964 when she went out in thirty.

CATHERINE LACOSTE, daughter of great French pre-war tennis ace René Lacoste and former British Ladies' golf champion Simone Thion de la Chaume, shook off the handicap of having parents who were famous in sport. She completed a unique collection of major title wins in 1969 when she won the French Open, British Open, United States Amateur and Spanish Open. Two years earlier she had won the U.S. Open against the best of the world's professionals. Born in Paris in 1945, she mastered the long irons and was noted for being a powerful and accurate hitter.

CAROL MANN, later Mrs Hardy, lifted women's golf to new heights of consistency and class in the 1960s. Born in Buffalo in 1941 and a professional from the age of twenty, she won ten tournaments in 1968 and eight the following year. Standing 6 feet 3 inches tall, she was a powerful player from the tee but could also play the short game with delicate skill. Her only major championship success came in the U.S. Open in 1965 and she was runner-up the following year. She became President of the U.S. LPGA in 1974.

KATHY WHITWORTH, born in Monahans, Texas in 1939, created history in women's golf when she became the first player to break through the million-dollar career-earnings barrier in 1981. A professional since 1959, she has had a record eighty-three official tournament victories since 1962. Deadly accurate from tee to green, she is devastating when facing pressure putts and had the best putting average in seven Tour seasons. She was Player of the Year seven times and leading money-winner for a record eight years. The only title to elude her was the U.S. Open.

JoANNE CARNER, born in Kirkland, Washington in 1939, turned professional after winning five U.S. Women's Amateur titles and in 1971, her first year on the pro circuit, she added the U.S. Women's Open to her collection. She had six wins on the Tour in 1974 and regained the Open title in 1976. By the early 1980s her career earnings had topped one million dollars and in 1982 she set an earnings record with a season's haul of 310,399 dollars. During 1982 she had twenty-five sub-70 rounds, equalling the record set by Amy Alcott in 1980. A feature of her play is her power with the long irons, which rival that of many top players on the men's circuit.

DONNA CAPONI, born in Detroit in 1945, has been a remarkably consistent player since turning professional in 1965. She has only once been out of the top thirty on the U.S. Tour and followed Kathy Whitworth and JoAnne Carner as the third woman to hit the million-dollar earnings target. Her first major championship victory was the U.S. Open in 1969. She clinched the title with a storm-interrupted final round of 69, the best in the event by a champion. The following year she joined Mickey Wright as the only player to retain the Open championship and on the way to the title she equalled Wright's Open aggregate record of 287. Her overseas successes included victory in the 1975 Colgate European Open and first place in the 1976 Australian Open, a title she won by a runaway margin of nine strokes.

MICHELLE WALKER, born at Alwoodley, Yorkshire in 1952, was Britain's most successful golfer in the 1970s. Undefeated in the 1972 Curtis Cup, she was the first British woman to win a major U.S. event for thirty-six years when she captured the 1972 U.S. Trans-Mississippi trophy. At eighteen, she became the youngest modern winner of the British Ladies' championship when she beat Beverly Huke in the 1971 final. She retained the title in 1972 with a two-hole victory over Claudine Rubin of France. She reached the final again in 1973 — her last year as an amateur — but was prevented fom completing a hat-trick by Ann Irvin who won by three and two at Carnoustie.

BETH DANIEL, born in Charleston in South Carolina, in 1956, won the U.S. Amateur title at her first attempt in 1975 when only eighteen. She regained the championship in 1977 before joining the professional Tour where her superb mid-irons play and exceptional putting has made her a major force. In only her second year on the pro circuit she won the World Ladies' championship in Japan and the following year she was the Tour's leading money-winner. She produced a brilliant aggregate total of 280 in the U.S. Open in 1981 but it was good enough only for second place behind Pat Bradley who won a thrilling duel by one stroke.

NANCY LOPEZ, later Mrs Knight and then Mrs Melton, was born in Torrance, California in 1957, and revealed early potential by winning the New Mexico Amateur title at the age of twelve. Her triumphs as a teenager included two U.S. Junior championships, the Mexican Amateur, three Western Junior Open titles and a runners-up place in the U.S. Open. She had an astonishing first year as a professional in 1978 when she won nine tournaments and a then record total of $189,813. Five of her seven wins on the U.S. Tour came in consecutive tournaments, a record run that gave women's golf a tremendous boost. She also captured the European Open and the Far East title in Japan. Nancy started to have problems with her swing in the 1980s but remained a leading player thanks to her power off the tee and her brilliant consistency with the putter.

JAN STEPHENSON, born in Sydney, Australia in 1951, but based in Fort Worth, Texas, proved she was ready to take her place in the front rank of women's golfers in the Mark Kay Classic at Dallas in 1981 when she shot 65−69−64 for victory and an astonishing

Nancy Lopez...made an astonishing professional debut

record-breaking eighteen-under-par total of 198. Two years later she won the U.S. Open with a 72–73–71–74 sequence to beat joint runners-up JoAnne Carner and Patty Sheehan by one stroke. An outstanding golfer from her early teens, she played more than two hundred successive tournaments as a professional without once missing the cut. She has brought glamour as well as her talent as a golfer to the pro Tour, and she appeared topless in the French magazine *Oui* after refusing offers to pose for *Playboy* and *Penthouse*.

HOLLIS STACY, born in Savannah, Georgia in 1954, won three consecutive U.S. Girls championships from 1969 to 1971 before joining the professional Tour. She captured the U.S. Open in 1977 with an aggregate 292, leading at the end of all four rounds and taking the title by two strokes from Nancy Lopez, with JoAnne Carner in third place. A year later she joined the select band of champions who have successfully defended the Open title and, at twenty-four, was the youngest to achieve the double.

AMY ALCOTT, born in Kansas City in 1956, was U.S. Junior champion in 1975 and won her first tournament as a professional in 1975 only five weeks after joining the Tour. Her peak performance came in the U.S. Open in 1980 when she broke the seventy-two-hole aggregate record by four strokes on the way to a sensational victory. She scorched round in temperatures topping over one hundred degrees, recording 70–70–68–72 for a final score of 280 and victory by nine strokes over runner-up Hollis Stacy. It was one of four victories for Amy in 1980 when she conjured twenty-five sub-70 rounds in official tournaments, an LPGA record.

PAT BRADLEY, born in Wesford, Massachusetts in 1951, turned professional in 1974 after dominating the amateur scene in her home state. After an indifferent start to her Tour career her confidence was boosted by victory in the Colgate Far East championship in Australia in 1975 and she suddenly began to establish herself as a force to be reckoned with. She had a thrilling last round head-to-head duel with Beth Daniel in the 1981 U.S. Open after appearing to be out of the hunt following opening rounds of 71 and 74 which put her six shots behind the leaders. She then produced third and fourth rounds of 66 and 68 to pip Beth Daniel by one stroke. This lowered by six shots the record total for the final thirty-six holes set by Mickey Wright twenty-two years earlier and her winning aggregate of 279 beat by one stroke the championship record set a year earlier by Amy Alcott.

SECTION FOUR
ALL KINDS OF EVERYTHING

WHO WOULD YOU HAVE PUTTING FOR YOUR LIFE?

During our research for *The Book of Golf Lists*, we asked the professionals which golfers they would like to have putting for them if their lives depended on it. These, in alphabetical order, were the putting kings who got most votes. They are not necessarily considered the finest putters but the men who, at their best, could be counted on to sink the vital putts when the pressure is at its peak.

GEORGE ARCHER *(USA)*
BILLY CASPER *(USA)*
BOB CHARLES *(New Zealand)*
BEN CRENSHAW *(USA)*
JIM FERRIER *(Australia)*
RAYMOND FLOYD *(USA)*
BEN HOGAN *(USA)*
BOBBY LOCKE *(South Africa)*
JACK NICKLAUS *(USA)*
ARNOLD PALMER *(USA)*
GARY PLAYER *(South Africa)*
BILL ROGERS *(USA)*
BOB ROSBURG *(USA)*
PETER THOMSON *(Australia)*
KEN VENTURI *(USA)*
TOM WATSON *(USA)*

THE MILLION-DOLLAR LEAGUE TABLE

Golf is one of the most financially rewarding of all sports — for the winners. This unofficial league table lists sixty of the golfers who have earned more than a million dollars in prize money:

More than $4,000,000
JACK NICKLAUS *(USA)*

More than $3,000,000
TOM WATSON *(USA)*
LEE TREVINO *(USA)*

More than $2,500,000
GARY PLAYER *(South Africa)*
HALE IRWIN *(USA)*
RAY FLOYD *(USA)*
JOHNNY MILLER *(USA)*
TOM WEISKOPF *(USA)*

More than $2,000,000
TOM KITE *(USA)*
ARNOLD PALMER *(USA)*
BILLY CASPER *(USA)*
GENE LITTLER *(USA)*
MILLER BARBER *(USA)*
ISAO AOKI *(Japan)*
BEN CRENSHAW *(USA)*
LANNY WADKINS *(USA)*
BRUCE LIETZKE *(USA)*
HUBERT GREEN *(USA)*

More than $1,500,000
SEVERIANO BALLESTEROS *(Spain)*
JERRY PATE *(USA)*
ANDY BEAN *(USA)*
BILL ROGERS *(USA)*

DAVID GRAHAM *(Australia)*
GIL MORGAN *(USA)*
CURTIS STRANGE *(USA)*
GRAHAM MARSH *(Australia)*
CRAIG STADLER *(USA)*
LARRY NELSON *(USA)*
GEORGE ARCHER *(USA)*
FUZZY ZOLLER *(USA)*
JOHN MAHAFFEY *(USA)*
J C SNEAD *(USA)*
AL GEIBERGER *(USA)*

More than $1,000,000

DON JANUARY *(USA)*
BRUCE CRAMPTON *(Australia)*
DAVE STOCKTON *(USA)*
LOU GRAHAM *(USA)*
CHARLES COODY *(USA)*
DAVE HILL *(USA)*
GAY BREWER *(USA)*
BOB MURPHY *(USA)*
GREG NORMAN *(Australia)*
JULIUS BOROS *(USA)*
FRANK BEARD *(USA)*
MASASHI OZAKI *(Japan)*
JIM COLBERT *(USA)*
TOMMY AARON *(USA)*
CALVIN PEETE *(USA)*
GEORGE BURNS *(USA)*
BRUCE DEVLIN *(Australia)*
WAYNE LEVI *(USA)*
JERRY McGEEE *(USA)*
JAY HAAS *(USA)*
BOB CHARLES *(New Zealand)*
JACK RENNER *(USA)*
CHI CHI RODRIGUEZ *(USA)*
LEE ELDER *(USA)*
DAN SIKES *(USA)*
LON HINKLE *(USA)*
BOBBY NICHOLS *(USA)*

A GAME FOR ALL AGES

ROBERTO DE VINCENZO, a winner of more than 240 tournaments during his forty-year globe-trotting career, was at forty-four years and ninety-three days the oldest winner of the Open championship cup when he won at Hoylake in 1967. **TOM MORRIS Snr** was forty-six years ninety-nine days old when he won the Open championship belt in 1867.

TOM MORRIS Jnr was seventeen years 249 days old when he won the Open championship belt in 1868. **WILLIE AUCHTERLONIE** was twenty-one years twenty-five days old when he captured the Open championship cup in 1893.

In 1968 at the age of forty-eight, **JULIUS BOROS** became the oldest man to win the U.S. PGA championship. Five years earlier he had become the oldest winner of the U.S. Open, his second triumph in that championship. Born in Connecticut in 1920, he did not turn professional until the age of thirty and over the next twenty years was a top contender in the major tournaments. He was a laconic, laid-back character who was the Perry Como of golf, often looking half asleep while waiting to take his shots. He once nodded off during an interview with a newspaperman and he often went missing at the end of his rounds and would be found fishing the ponds on the course. Julius always packed his fishing rod before his golf clubs.

GARY PLAYER was, at twenty-three, the youngest British Open champion of the century when he captured the title at Muirfield in 1959. **SEVERIANO BALLESTEROS** took over as the youngest Open champion of the century when he won at Royal Lytham in 1979 at the age of twenty-two years 103 days.

ALEX (SANDY) HERD, British Open champion in 1902, was fifty-eight when he won the British Professional Match Play championship in 1923. **JAMES BRAID** was fifty-seven when he finished runner-up the following year.

HARRY VARDON was fifty when he finished equal second in the 1920 U.S. Open, just a stroke behind compatriot Ted Ray who was forty-three.

SAM SNEAD was fifty-two when he won the Greater Greensboro Open in 1965 and sixty-two when he finished equal third in the U.S. PGA championship in 1974. **DAI REES** was sixty when he finished second in the Martini International in 1973.

Gary Player...winner of the British Open at twenty-three

HENRY COTTON, three times Open champion (1934–37–48), was fifty when he tied for sixth place in the Open at Hoylake in 1956.

FRANCIS OUIMET was unknown outside his home state of Massachusetts when he won the U.S. Open in 1913 at the age of twenty. He forced a tie with powerful British duo Harry Vardon and Ted Ray and then won the play-off to end the domination of the U.S. Open by British players and Scottish immigrants. His victory made front-page news and opened the way for the rapid development of the game in the United States. In 1951-52 he was elected captain of the Royal and Ancient Golf Club, the first non-Briton to receive the honour.

The Hon. **MICHAEL SCOTT** won the British Amateur championship at Hoylake in 1933 at the age of fifty-four. **JOHN BEHARRELL** and **BOBBY COLE** were both eighteen years one month old when they won the Amateur title in 1956 and 1966 respectively. **NICK FALDO** (1975) and **PAUL DOWNES** (1978) were both eighteen when they won the English Amateur championship.

MAY HEZLET was the youngest winner of the British Ladies' championship. She was just a week past her seventeenth birthday when she won in 1899. Mrs **JESSE VALENTINE** won the British Ladies' Amateur Open in 1958 at the age of forty-three.

MICHELLE WALKER won the British Ladies' championship in 1971 when eighteen. Her opponent in the final, Beverly Huke, was twenty. **JANET MELVILLE** was, at twenty, the youngest winner of the British Ladies' Open stroke-play title in 1978.

ALL-STAR ALL STARS

Which star signs produce the best golfers? Judge for yourself from the following all-star birthday lists:

CAPRICORN
December 22 – January 20

Michael Bonallack (GB)
31.12.34
Cary Middlecoff (USA)
6.1.21
Lou Graham (USA)
7.1.38
Ken Brown (GB)
9.1.57
Ben Crenshaw (USA)
11.1.52
Graham Marsh (Aus)
14.1.44

AQUARIUS
January 21 – February 19

Jack Nicklaus (USA)
21.1.40
Henry Cotton (GB)
26.1.07
Byron Nelson (USA)
4.2.12
Sandy Lyle (GB)
9.2.58
Greg Norman (Aus)
10.2.55
Norman von Nida (Aus)
14.2.14

PISCES
February 20 – March 20

Gene Sarazen (USA)
27.2.02
Peter Alliss (GB)
28.2.31
Julius Boros (USA)
3.3.20
Bob Goalby (USA)
14.3.29
Bob Charles (NZ)
14.3.36
Gay Brewer (USA)
19.3.32

ARIES
March 21 – April 20

Ed Furgol (USA)
22.3.17
Peter Butler (GB)
25.3.32
Tommy Bolt (USA)
31.3.18
Phil Rodgers (USA)
3.4.38
Seve Ballesteros (Sp)
9.4.57
Roberto de Vicenzo (Arg)
14.4.23

TAURUS
April 21—May 21

John Fallon *(GB)*
29.4.13
Johnny Miller *(USA)*
29.4.47
Peter Oosterhuis *(GB)*
3.5.48
Bobby Cole *(SA)*
11.5.48
Ken Venturi *(USA)*
15.5.31
Dave Hill *(USA)*
20.5.37

GEMINI
May 22—June 21

David Graham *(Aus)*
23.5.46
Sam Snead *(USA)*
27.5.12
Johnny Bulla *(USA)*
2.6.14
Brian Barnes *(GB)*
3.6.45
Hale Irwin *(USA)*
3.6.45
Tommy Horton *(GB)*
16.6.41

CANCER
June 22—July 23

Flory van Donck *(Bel)*
23.6.12
Billy Casper *(USA)*
24.6.31
Clive Clark *(GB)*
27.6.45
Tony Jacklin *(GB)*
7.7.44
Nick Faldo *(GB)*
18.7.57
Gene Littler *(USA)*
21.7.30

LEO
July 24—August 23

Doug Sanders *(USA)*
24.7.33
Max Faulkner *(GB)*
29.7.16
Frank Stranahan *(USA)*
5.8.22
Ben Hogan *(USA)*
13.8.12
Dave Thomas *(GB)*
16.8.34
Peter Thomson *(Aus)*
23.8.29

VIRGO
August 24 – September 23

Bernhard Langer *(Ger)*
27.8.57
Raymond Floyd *(USA)*
4.9.42
Tom Watson *(USA)*
4.9.49
Arnold Palmer *(USA)*
10.9.29
Bill Rogers *(USA)*
10.9.51
Jerry Pate *(USA)*
16.9.53

LIBRA
September 24 – October 23

Neil Coles *(GB)*
26.9.34
Bruce Crampton *(Aus)*
28.9.35
George Archer *(USA)*
1.10.39
Ken Bousfield *(GB)*
2.10.19
Harold Henning *(SA)*
3.10.34
Fred Daly *(GB)*
11.10.11

SCORPIO
October 24 – November 22

Gary Player *(SA)*
1.11.35
Dave Stockton *(USA)*
2.11.49
Tom Weiskopf *(USA)*
9.11.42
Fuzzy Zoeller *(USA)*
11.11.51
Bobby Locke *(SA)*
20.11.17
Brian Huggett *(GB)*
18.11.36

SAGITTARIUS
November 23 – December 21

Lee Trevino *(USA)*
1.12.39
Lanny Wadkins *(USA)*
5.12.49
Orville Moody *(USA)*
9.12.33
Tom Kite *(USA)*
9.12.49
Kel Nagle *(Aus)*
21.12.20
Christy O'Connor *(Irl)*
21.12.24

RAY REARDON
How I Would Like To Play the Game

I would consider myself the perfect golfer if I could have...

The **DRIVE** of **GREG NORMAN**
The **SWING** of **SEVE BALLESTEROS**
The **LONG IRONS** game of **LEE TREVINO**
The **SHORT IRONS** game of **TOM WATSON**
The **BUNKER SHOTS** of **TONY JACKLIN**
The **PUTTING** of **NICK FALDO**
The **TEMPERAMENT** of **JACK NICKLAUS**

'I think the golfer who has come nearest to being perfect is Tom Watson, and Seve Ballesteros is well on the way to being just as good if not better. I had the pleasure of playing with Seve at Gleneagles once and, even though it was pouring with rain, I enjoyed every second of it. He's a magnificent master of the game.'

RAY REARDON has been world snooker champion six times and has won thousands of followers for his sport with his skilled performances and pleasant, unassuming personality. His passion away from the snooker table is golf and he plays off a sixteen handicap.

HAPPY FAMILIES

Relatively speaking, golf is a great family game. These are among the most successful golfing families...

'OLD TOM' and **'YOUNG TOM' MORRIS** monopolized the Open championship in the first twelve years of its existence. First of all 'Old Tom', born in North Street, St Andrews in 1821, won it four times to three by his arch rival Willie Park between 1861 and 1867. Then 'Young Tom' came on to the scene, winning the championship belt four times in succession before his tragic death at the age of twenty-four on Christmas Day 1875. It was said that he died of a broken heart following the death of his wife and her new-born baby.

WILLIE PARK, the first Open champion in 1860, won his fourth Open in 1875 and his son, Willie Jnr, triumphed in 1887 and 1889. **MUNGO PARK**, Willie's brother who was a seaman, stayed on land long enough to win the Open in 1874. Willie Jnr's daughter Doris (later Mrs Porter) played regularly for Scotland between the two world wars.

WILLIE AUCHTERLONIE won the British Open at Prestwick in 1893. Nine years later his older brother, Laurence – a native of St Andrew's but representing the Chicago Golf Club – won the U.S. Open at Garden City.

TOM VARDON was runner-up to his famous brother Harry in the 1903 Open championship at Prestwick.

The **SMITH** brothers of Scotland – Alex, Willie and MacDonald – had an extraordinary record in the U.S. Open. Both Willie (1899) and Alex (1906 and 1910) won the title and MacDonald tied for first place in 1910, but finished third in a three-way play-off won by his brother Alex.

The **WHITCOMBE** brothers were prominent on the British golf circuit between the two world wars. Ernest, the eldest, was runner-up to Walter Hagen in the 1923 Open at Hoylake and Reggie won the 1938 Open at Royal St George's. Ernest, Reggie and another brother, Charles, were all members of the 1935 Ryder Cup team.

Brothers **SID** and **JOCK BREWS** between them won twelve South African Open championships. **GEORGE FOTHERINGHAM** won the South African Open five times between 1908 and 1914, with his brother **JOHN** interrupting his winning sequence in 1909.

Brother and sister **ROGER** and **JOYCE WETHERED** learned their golf together at Dornoch where their father had a holiday house. Roger was an outstanding amateur who lost to Jock Hutchison in a play-off for the British Open in 1921. Joyce, later Lady Heathcoat-Amory, dominated English ladies' golf in the 1920s.

PERCY ALLISS won twenty major tournaments including the British Match Play championship in 1933 and 1937. His son, Peter — born in 1931 in Berlin where Percy was a club professional — became an outstanding international golfer and renowned course designer, and he is now the 'Voice of Golf' on BBC television. Both Percy and Peter played in the Ryder Cup. Alec, Peter's older brother, was also a good-class professional.

HARRY and **ARNOLD BENTLEY** are the only brothers to have won the English Amateur championship, Harry in 1936 and Arnold in 1939.

MICHAEL BONALLACK, present Secretary of the Royal and Ancient Golf Club, was one of the greatest amateur golfers of all time. He dominated the British Amateur championship throughout the 1960s and was an outstanding Walker Cup contestant and captain. His wife, formerly Angela Ward, twice won the English women's championship and his sister, Sally, also won the title. Michael was a county-class cricketer but elected to concentrate on golf after winning the Boys' championship in 1952.

The five **HENNING** brothers were all leading golfers in South Africa. Harold, Alan and Graham all joined the world professional tour, with Harold the best known and the most successful.

Five **TURNESA** brothers followed their teaching-professional father on to the American golf circuit. Two of them, Joe and Jim, represented the United States in the Ryder Cup and Willie — a former British and American Amateur champion — played in three Walker Cup matches.

The **TOOGOOD** family dominated the Tasmanian Open in 1956. Brothers Peter and John finished first and third, with their father Alf in second place. Two years earlier Peter and John were first and second in the Australian Amateur championship.

JAY and **LIONEL HERBERT**, Louisiana professionals, are the only brothers to have won the U.S. PGA championship – Jay in 1960 and Lionel, five years younger, in 1957.

BOBBY and **LANNY WADKINS** are prominent professionals in the United States. Lanny won the U.S. PGA championship in 1977 and the following year his younger brother Bobby became the first European Open champion.

CATHY PANTON was following in her father's footsteps when she won the British Women's Amateur championship in 1978 before switching to the professional circuit. John Panton was for many years one of Scotland's leading professionals.

CHRISTY O'CONNOR Jnr is following in his uncle's footsteps as a top-quality golf professional. Between 1959 and 1969, Christy Sr finished in the top six in the Open championship on seven occasions and in 1965 came second two shots behind Peter Thomson. His nephew was Britain's joint leading player in the 1976 Open when he finished fifth. Both O'Connors were born in Galway – Senior in 1924 and Junior in 1948.

JESSE SNEAD, nephew of Slammin' Sam, followed his illustrious uncle into the U.S. Ryder Cup team.

SEVERIANO BALLESTEROS is the youngest and best of four professional golfing brothers, and they are all nephews of Ramon Sota who was one of the great pioneers of Spanish professional golf.

ANGEL MIGUEL succeeded his brother Sebastian as Spanish Open champion in 1961 and together they were runners-up for Spain in the 1958 World Cup tournament in Mexico.

Irishman **JOE CARR** was one of the finest amateur golfers in Europe, winning the Irish championship six times and the British Amateur title three times. He was a regular member of the Walker Cup team. His son, Roddy, followed him into the Walker Cup team and was on the winning side against the United States in 1971 before joining the professional ranks. John Carr, another of Joe's sons, has also played for Ireland.

BERNARD HUNT beat his brother Geoffrey in the 1953 final of the British Assistants championship at Hartsbourne, where Geoffrey later followed his father as club professional. Both Bernard and Geoffrey played in the 1963 Ryder Cup.

WHAT A CARRY ON!

The term 'caddie' derives from the French word *cadet* meaning 'attendant'. Mary Queen of Scots, who played golf while being schooled in France, is the reputed source of the name. Here is a collection of true stories about golfing caddies who carry on regardless:

The advice of a good caddie can often mean the difference between victory and defeat for a golfer. **Gay Brewer** proved that he appreciated the truth of this by twice tipping his caddie Alfie Fyles £1,000 when winning the Alcan Golfer of the Year title in successive years.

Alfie Fyles was raised in Suffolk Road close to Royal Birkdale — a road that could be called Champions Way. Fyles has caddied four times for British Open winners — once for Gary Player and in three triumphs with Tom Watson. His brother, Albert, caddied for Tom Weiskopf when he won the Open and their Suffolk Road neighbours Jacky Leigh (twice for Peter Thompson) and Teddy Dalsall (for Johnny Miller) have shouldered the responsibility as caddies in Open championship victories.

Max Faulkner, the 1951 Open champion, employed a regular caddie nicknamed 'Mad Mac' who was, to say the least, somewhat eccentric. He wore a raincoat but no shirt and always studied the greens through binoculars from which the lenses had been removed. He once advised Faulkner: 'Hit this putt slightly straight, sir.'

Faulkner, one of the most colourful golfers ever to set foot on a course, was teeing off in a domestic tournament when he noticed his caddie swaying as if in a strong wind. 'Are you all right?' he asked. 'I'm trim as a daisy,' the caddie replied with a slurred voice. 'I've just finished a bottle of brandy and will start on the next one when you've won this tournament.' Faulkner birdied the hole in two and then looked around for the flag. His caddie was flat out on the side of the green clasping the flag in his arms. He replaced the flag in the hole and then half carried and half dragged the caddie behind a gorse bush where he left him sleeping like a baby.

Walter Travis, first American winner of the British Amateur championship in 1904, was accompanied throughout the tournament by a caddie who was described as 'a cross-eyed half wit'. During Travis's second-round match against James Robb the caddie walked on to the eleventh green and picked up the wrong ball before a putt had been made. Travis demanded a change of caddie but was ignored. There is perhaps truth in the rumour that, when asked his handicap, Travis replied: 'My caddie.'

Julius Boros was once penalized two strokes after his caddie had picked up his ball and tossed it to him. Somebody in the gallery had shouted 'That's good' and the caddie thought it was Boros's opponent giving him the putt.

British caddie **John Allen** worked in a casino until he started accompanying American champion Billy Casper, a devout Mormon. He had such an impact on Allen that he adopted the Mormon faith and became a regular member of the Casper entourage on golfing trips around the world.

James Robb, British Amateur champion in 1906, hooked his ball at the eleventh hole in the final of the British Amateur at Muirfield in 1897. The ball was found in his caddie's pocket and Robb had to forfeit the hole to eventual champion Jack Allan.

Frank Stranahan found just how sensitive some caddies can be during the British Amateur championship at Troon in 1956. On one hole he selected a club different to that advised by his veteran Scottish caddie who deliberately gave him a wrong line so that he fired the ball into thick gorse. The caddie then threw down the golf bag and declared: 'If you canna bother usin' what I tell yer, then carry the bloomin' bag yesel'.' He then marched off the course.

Bobby Brue quickly realized he had been given a novice caddie during a tournament on the American Tour. After driving from the first tee he asked the caddie how far he was from the green. The caddie gave careful consideration before replying: 'I'd say about three blocks.'

Each year when the new Royal and Ancient Golf Club captain 'tees off' into office, a cannon is fired and the caddie who retrieves the ball is given a golden sovereign.

Orville Moody once had a caddie who went to extremes to be exact in his measurements. He even used to walk through water hazards with the golf bag held above his head, to be sure he got the distances right.

Singer **Andy Williams**, a golf fanatic, was having one of those rounds when nothing would go right in a charity tournament in Atlanta. He was in and out of the woods on one hole and on reaching the green asked his caddie: 'What should I do with this putt?' The caddie advised: 'Keep it as low as possible.'

Tommy Bolt, notorious for his short temper on the golf course, once snapped a six-iron across his thigh after mishitting an approach shot to the green. His caddie, in an equal rage, grabbed a five-iron from the bag, snapped it and then walked off the course.

Doug Sanders's putting let him down in the 1968 Masters during a round when he played magnificent golf everywhere except on the greens. At the end of the round his caddie, **Walter 'Cricket' Pritchett** who was famous for his one-liners, said: 'Nice work, Mister Doug. You've just turned a perfect 64 into a 72.' Sanders once had a novice caddie who when asked after a drive how far it was to get home replied: 'I wish I could tell you, sir, but I don't even know where you live.'

HOW EVEN THE MIGHTY CAN FALL

Here's a list that will give heart to all those golfers who know what it is to visit every part of a course on the way to treble figures. Even the mightiest golfers can be cut down to size.

WILLIE FERNIE included a ten on his card while on his way to the Open championship at Musselburgh in 1883. It's the only time an Open champion has had double figures on his card. He made amends on the final hole of a play-off for the title against Bob Ferguson, chipping in from off the green for an eagle two.

TOMMY ARMOUR came down to earth with a crash the week after winning the U.S. Open in 1927. Competing in the Shawnee Open, Armour took twenty-three strokes on the seventeenth. He had been experimenting with a hooked drive and sent a procession of balls out of bounds.

TOM WEISKOPF had a nightmare twelfth hole in the first round of the U.S. Masters in 1980. He hit his ball into the water hazard five times and finally took a thirteen at the par-three hole...which sunk his hopes out of sight.

BEN CRENSHAW was also drowning his sorrows in the third round of the 1976 World Series at Firestone. He dropped three successive wedge shots into the lake in front of the sixteenth green and finally got down in eleven.

BRIAN BARNES was within four feet of the hole in three strokes on the short eighth hole in the French Open at St Cloud in 1968. He finished with a fifteen after a nightmare series of snatched putts plus penalty strokes for standing astride the line of a putt.

HERMAN TISSIES, German Amateur champion in 1949, was leading the qualifiers for the British Open at Royal Troon the following year until he came up against the notorious 126-yard 'Postage Stamp' eighth hole. He missed the green with his tee-shot and then kept hitting the ball backwards and forwards across the green from bunker to bunker. He finally single-putted for fifteen!

FRANK WALSH, competing in the U.S. Masters in 1935, had a disaster at the twelfth hole when he took twelve strokes to get down.

Ben Crenshaw...felt like drowning his sorrows

SAM SNEAD appeared to have a jinx on him in the U.S. Open. It was the one major championship that eluded him throughout his distinguished career and he was runner-up four times. His best chance of winning came in 1939 when he stood on the final tee needing just a six to win. Wrong information was fed to Snead and he was under the impression he needed a par five. He went for prodigious recovery shots after getting himself into trouble on the fairway and finished with a nightmare eight.

BOBBY LOCKE, four times British Open champion, waved goodbye to the title in a bunker on the third hole at Hoylake in 1956. The great man took three to get out of the sand and finished with an eight that wrecked his victory chances. He returned the following year to regain the championship at St Andrews.

DAVE HILL, runner-up in the U.S. Open in 1970, blew his chances in the 1962 U.S. Open at Oakmont when he six-putted the fifth green.

JACK NICKLAUS had a long, hard look at the feared eleventh 'Railway' hole at Royal Troon in the 1962 Open — too long and too hard! He spent most of his time looking for his ball in the rough and finished with a ten on his way to a round of 80. Max Faulkner, 1951 Open champion, also came to grief at the double dogleg eleventh — with an eleven.

TSUNEUKI NAKAJIMA must have felt he was in sinking sands when he put his third stroke — a mishit putt — into the bunker on the dreaded 'Road' hole at St Andrews in the 1978 Open. It took him a frustrating five shots to escape from the bunker and he finished with a nine to wreck his dreams of winning the Open.

BOBBY CLAMPETT was running away with the British Open at Royal Troon in 1982 until — in the third round — he came to the marathon sixth hole, at 577 yards the longest hole in British championship golf. He found a bunker with his drive, played out into another bunker and then made his way via the rough to the green where he two-putted for a disastrous eight. Clampett faded away to joint tenth.

IT TAKES ALL SORTS

BRUCE DEVLIN *(Australia)* used to be a plumber

JULIUS BOROS *(USA)* was an accountant

TONY JACKLIN *(Great Britain)* was a steamfitter's apprentice

CARY MIDDLECOFF *(USA)* qualified as a dentist

ORVILLE MOODY *(USA)* served for fourteen years in the U.S. Army

PETER THOMSON *(Australia)* was an industrial chemist

GRAHAM MARSH *(Australia)* was a maths teacher

JACK NEWTON *(Australia)* was a P.E. teacher

SIMON HOBDAY *(Zimbabwe)* was a farmer and then a car salesman

LEE TREVINO *(USA)* spent four years in the U.S. Marines

GIL MORGAN *(USA)* qualified as a doctor of optometry

JUAN RODRIGUEZ *(Puerto Rico)* used to be a shoeshine boy

JAMES BRAID *(Great Britain)* worked as a plasterer

DAVID BROWN *(Great Britain)* was a roof slater

IAN COLDWELL *(Great Britain)* is a Harley Street dentist

TOM WATSON *(USA)* graduated in psychology from Stanford University

FROM ALL WALKS OF LIFE

What the fathers of fifteen great golfers did for a living...

GRAVEDIGGER (Lee Trevino)
BLACKSMITH (Ben Hogan)
BLACKSMITH (Walter Hagen)
GOLDMINE SUPERINTENDENT (Gary Player)
GARDENER (Francis Ouimet)
FARMER (Seve Ballesteros)
GREENKEEPER (Arnold Palmer)
PHARMACIST (Jack Nicklaus)
GAMEKEEPER (Harry Weetman)
UNIVERSITY PROFESSOR (Freddie Tait)
STONEMASON (Alex Ross)
PLOUGHMAN (James Braid)
CARPENTER (Gene Sarazen)
FARMER (Christy O'Connor Snr)
SHOE REPAIR SHOPS' OWNER (Neil Coles)

TOM GRAVENEY
How I Would Like To Play the Game

I would consider myself the perfect golfer if I could have...

The **DRIVE** of **TONY JACKLIN**
The **SWING** of **NICK FALDO**
The **LONG IRONS** game of **JACK NICKLAUS**
The **SHORT IRONS** game of **SEVE BALLESTEROS**
The **BUNKER SHOTS** of **GARY PLAYER**
The **PUTTING** of **BOB CHARLES**
The **TEMPERAMENT** of **PETER THOMSON**

'I agonized over having to leave out Bobby Locke and, of course, the great Henry Cotton about whom I have heard and read so much but never actually saw play. To my mind, the player who has come nearest to achieving perfection on the golf course is Tom Watson. If I had just a little of the talent of the players I have selected I think I would perhaps start winning a few games.'

TOM GRAVENEY was the first batsman to score a century of centuries in post-war cricket. A master off his front foot, he was a thoughtful tactician who captained Gloucestershire, Worcestershire and England. He is a respected member of the BBC TV commentary team and takes every opportunity when not at the microphone to improve his golf. He plays off seven.

THE LONG, THE SHORT AND THE TALL

Golf champions come in all shapes and sizes. This is how a selection of a gallery of great golfers measure up...

GEORGE ARCHER, at 6 feet 7 inches, was the tallest pro on the U.S. circuit in the 1960s and 70s. He was U.S. Masters champion in 1969. **CAROL MANN**, 1965 U.S. Women's Open champion, stands 6 feet 3 inches or, as she herself says, 'five feet fifteen inches'.

GENE SARAZEN, winner of the Big Four championships in 1932, was 5 feet 5 inches tall.

JAMES BRAID was a tall, wiry 6 feet 1½ inches and weighed 12st (168lbs); **J.H. TAYLOR** stood 5 feet 8½ inches and weighed 11st 7lbs (161lbs); **HARRY VARDON** was 5 feet 9½ inches tall and weighed 11st (154lbs).

FRED McLEOD, Scots-born winner of the U.S. Open in 1908, stood 5 feet 5 inches and weighed just 7st 10lb (108lbs).

GARY PLAYER stands just 5 feet 7 inches tall; **ARNOLD PALMER** is 5 feet 10½ inches and at his peak weighed 13st 8llbs (190lbs).

TOM WEISKOPF, British Open champion in 1973, stands 6 feet 4 inches.

DAVE THOMAS, twice runner-up in the British Open, stands 6 feet 2 inches and weighs 15st.

PETER OOSTERHUIS, runner-up in the 1974 British Open, stands 6 feet 5 inches and weighs 15st 7lb (217lbs).

OLIN DUTRA, winner of the U.S. Open in 1934, stood 6 feet 5 inches.

ANDY NORTH, winner of the U.S. Open in 1978, stands 6 feet 4 inches.

CRAIG STADLER, 1982 U.S. Masters champion, stands 5 feet 10 inches and is a beefy 15st 4lbs (214lbs)

JUAN (CHI CHI) RODRIGUEZ, a million-dollar earner from Puerto Rico, stands 5 feet 7 inches and weighs just 7st 10lbs (108lbs).

WILLIE MILNE, a professional from Perth and a former Walker Cup player, stands 6 feet 3 inches and weighs 17st 4lbs (242lbs).

SUKREE ONSHAM, champion of Thailand who was third in the World Cup individual tournament in 1969, stood fractionally under 5 feet 2 inches and weighed barely 8st (112lbs).

GEORGE BAYER, the 1957 Canadian Open champion who is regarded as the longest hitter of a ball on the post-war circuit, stands 6 feet 5 inches and weighs in at more than 17st (238lbs).

Australia's highly-rated **JIM FERRIER**, whose distinguished career bridged the Second World War, was a towering 6 feet 4 inches. **NORMAN VON NIDA**, outstanding in the immediate post-war years, was a 5 feet 5 inches 9st featherweight, and the latest star from Down Under, **GREG NORMAN**, is 6 feet 1 inch and weighs in at 13st 6lbs (188lbs).

GREAT SCOTS

Scotland gave golf to the world and has produced a procession of great golfers to help spread the gospel. These are sixty of the great Scots who have distinguished themselves in golf. The asterisk denotes golfers who emigrated to the United States and the double asterisk denotes the golfers who won the British Open championship.

Jimmy Adams *(Troon, 1910)*
Willie Anderson *(North Berwick, 1878)**
Jamie Anderson *(St Andrews, 1842)***
Tommy Armour *(Edinburgh, 1895)****
Laurie Auchterlonie *(St Andrews, 1868)**
Willie Auchterlonie *(St Andrews, 1872)***
Harry Bannerman *(Aberdeen, 1942)*
Brian Barnes *(Addington, 1945)*
Ted Blackwell *(St Andrews, 1866)*
David Blair *(Nairn, 1917)*
James Braid *(Earls-Ferry, 1870)***
Gordon Brand Jnr *(Kirkcaldy, 1958)*
David Brown *(Musselburgh, 1869)***
Eric Brown *(Edinburgh, 1925)*
Ken Brown *(Harpenden, 1957)*
William Campbell *(Musselburgh, 1862)***
Bobby Cruickshank *(Granton-on-Spey, 1894)**
Findlay Douglas *(St Andrews, 1875)**
George Duncan *(Methlick, 1883)***
Willie Dunn Snr *(Musselburgh, 1821)*
Willie Dunn Jnr *(Musselburgh, 1865)*
John Fallon *(Lanark, 1913)*
Bob Ferguson *(Musselburgh, 1848)***
Willie Fernie *(St Andrews, 1851)***
James Foulis *(St Andrews, 1868)**
Bernard Gallacher *(Bathgate, 1949)*
Tom Haliburton *(Wentworth, 1915)*
Sandy Herd *(St Andrews, 1868)***
Jock Hutchison *(St Andrews, 1884)****

Sandy Lyle...born in England but a proud Scot

David Ingram *(Huntly, 1945)*

Tom Kidd *(St Andrews, 1845)*

Andrew Kirkaldy *(Denhead, 1860)*

Hugh Kirkaldy *(Denhead, 1865)***

Johnny Laidlay *(Seacliff, 1860)*

George Low *(Carnoustie, 1874)**

Sandy Lyle *(Shrewsbury, 1958)*

Willie McFarlane *(Aberdeen, 1890)**

Freddie McLeod *(North Berwick, 1882)**

Bob Martin *(St Andrews, 1848)***

Tom Morris Snr *(St Andrews, 1821)***

Tom Morris Jnr *(St Andrews, 1851)***

John Panton *(Pitlochry, 1916)*

Mungo Park Snr *(Musselburgh, 1839)***

Willie Park Snr *(Musselburgh, 1834)***

Willie Park Jnr *(Musselburgh, 1864)***

Allan Robertson *(St Andrews, 1815)*

Alex Ross *(Dornoch, 1881)*

Ben Sayers *(Leith, 1857)*

Ronnie Shade *(Edinburgh, 1918)*

Andrew Shaw *(Troon, 1898)†*

Alex Smith *(Carnoustie, 1872)**

Macdonald Smith *(Carnoustie, 1890)**

Willie Smith *(Carnoustie, 1875)**

Andrew Strath *(St Andrews, 1836)***

Freddie Tait *(Dalkeith, 1870)*

Jimmy Thomson *(North Berwick, 1908)**

Sam Torrance *(Largs, 1953)*

Jack White *(North Berwick, 1873)***

George Will *(Ladybank, 1937)*

Norman Wood *(Prestonpans, 1947)*

***Jock Hutchison and Tommy Armour won the British Open after emigrating to the United States.

†Andrew Shaw emigrated to New Zealand after the First World War and won the New Zealand Open five times between 1926 and 1936.

Note: Brian Barnes, Ken Brown and Sandy Lyle were born in England but choose to represent Scotland.

BACK FROM THE DEAD

There have been many extraordinary comebacks in the hotly competitive world of match play golf. These are among the most famous.

GARY PLAYER's great fighting spirit was never more in evidence than when he beat Tony Lema in the Piccadilly World Match Play championship at Wentworth in 1965 after being seven down with seventeen to play. Player overheard two spectators chatting as he walked towards the twentieth tee. One said to his companion that they should wait for the next match because this one would soon be over. The super-confident South African paused and said: 'Sir, you are obviously not a golfer or you would know that a game is never over until it's lost. Stick around and you might see something.' He then proceeded to unwrap one of the greatest comebacks in golfing history. He squared the match on the thirty-sixth and won it on the thirty-seventh. He went on to beat Peter Thomson in the final.

American amateur **DONALD MOE** was seven down with thirteen holes left to play against Britain's J.A. Stout in a 1930 thirty-six-hole Walker Cup match at Sandwich. Moe pulled level at the seventh (the thirty-fifth hole of the match) and birdied the last for a round of 67 and victory by one hole.

George Voigt and Harry Girvan were seven up with eleven to play in their 1936 Walker Cup match against British pair **ALEC HILL** and **CECIL EWING** at Pine Valley in 1936. A marvellous fight back by Hill and Ewing saw them all square with one to play. The remaining hole and the match was halved.

Edinburgh-born **BOBBY CRUIKSHANK** staged a remarkable recovery in the days when the U.S. PGA championship was decided by match play. He eliminated Al Watrous after being eleven down with twelve to play.

BOBBY LOCKE was four down with six to play in the first important final of his career, the 1935 Transvaal Amateur championship. He holed a long putt and saw his opponent betray emotions that revealed a lack of confidence even though he was three up with five to play. This boosted his confidence and he battled on to win the match at the nineteenth. He said in later years that he learned a valuable lesson from this match – 'never reveal any sort of emotion on the golf course that can give confidence or comfort to your opponent.'

BILLY CASPER won the 1969 Alcan 'Golfer of the Year' championship at Portland after looking doomed to defeat against Lee Trevino. With three holes to play, Trevino was leading by six shots. Casper birdied the last three holes, while Trevino dropped three shots at the short par-three seventeenth to let his opponent in for an astonishing victory.

Three years earlier, Casper had staged one of the most remarkable recoveries in a major stroke-play tournament to win the 1966 U.S. Open. With nine holes to go he was trailing the great Arnold Palmer by seven strokes but pulled back for a tie. Casper was four strokes down in the play-off but fought back for an incredible victory that is perhaps unkindly remembered as the title that Palmer lost rather than the one that battling Billy won.

JUST ONE OF THOSE THINGS

Every golfer dreams of scoring a hole-in-one and it's surprising how many find their dreams come true. Just in 1981 alone the American magazine *Golf Digest* recorded 35,757 holes-in-one in the United States – an average of ninety a day.

There have been several instances of a hole-in-one in the British Open but **CHARLES WARD**, of Little Aston, is the only golfer who has achieved two aces. He holed out at the eighth in the Open at St Andrew's in 1946 on his way to finishing in fourth place. Two years later at Muirfield he holed-in-one at the thirteenth and finally tied for third place.

TOM MORRIS Jnr recorded the first hole-in-one in a major championship when he holed out at the 145-yard eighth at Prestwick in the 1868 Open.

JAMIE ANDERSON was about to tee off at the seventeenth in the 1878 Open at Prestwick when he was told he was outside the teeing ground and risked disqualification. He replaced the ball and holed-in-one and went on to win the championship by one stroke.

TONY JACKLIN performed the first hole-in-one on television when he aced at the sixteenth at Royal St George's, Sandwich, on his way to a round of 64 and victory in the 1967 Dunlop Masters. Jacklin was bang on target again in the 1978 German Open when his hole-in-one won him a Mercedes sports car.

LIONEL PLATTS, former British Ryder Cup golfer, had the television cameras trained on him when he holed-in-one at the 212-yard fourth in the 1971 Open at Royal Birkdale.

In 1973 **GENE SARAZEN**, seventy-one years young, holed-in-one at the 'Postage Stamp' eighth at Troon – fifty years after making his debut in the Open on the same course where he had a nightmare 85. Amateur **DAVID RUSSELL** also aced at the eighth in the 1973 Open at Troon.

There were a record *three* holes-in-one at the 1981 Open at Sandwich, all at the short 165-yard sixth. **GORDON BRAND** was first to ace in the second round, using a five-iron. The next day amateur **ROGER CHAPMAN** took a nine-iron and was down in

Gene Sarazen...a happy return with a hole-in-one

one. Then on the final day **SAM TORRANCE** holed out with his tee-shot, using a six-iron.

JERRY McGEE and **BOBBY MITCHELL** both holed-in-one at the 180-yard fifth in the 1972 U.S. Open at Pebble Beach.

PETER BUTLER scored the first hole-in-one in a Ryder Cup match when he aced at the 188-yard sixteenth at Muirfield in 1973.

ISAO AOKI holed-in-one at the second against David Graham in the 1979 Suntory World Match Play championship at Wentworth and was rewarded with a Bovis home at Gleneagles valued at £55,000. It became known as the 'home-in-one' shot.

DICK KOLBUS, from Oakland, California, won a Rolls-Royce for holing-in-one at the 105-yard fourteenth in the 1965 Harrah Invitational Tournament at the Tahoe Paradise course.

WILLIE MILNE, former Walker Cup player from Scotland before turning professional, thought he had won a Mercedes car when he holed-in-one during the 1979 French Open. The tournament organizers then announced that the car offer had been withdrawn. Milne, who stands 6 feet 3 inches and weighs in at more than 17st, didn't take the matter into his own hands but turned it over to his solicitors and after a long wrangle finally got the motor car.

DON JANUARY, 1967 U.S. PGA champion, collected $50,000 for a hole-in-one at Palm Springs in 1961.

South African **HAROLD HENNING** holed-in-one at the eighteenth in the 1963 Esso Golden tournament at Moor Park and collected a prize of £10,000. His caddie, Denis Hutchinson, was just as pleased and excited as Henning. Along with another South African, Trevor Wilkes, they were sharing all expenses and all winnings. So the hole-in-one prize was split three ways.

HARRY WEETMAN, a major force in British golf over two decades following the Second World War, clinched victory in the Assistants' championship at Worsley in 1950 when he holed his tee shot at the 172-yard eighteenth in the final round of the seventy-two-hole tournament.

ROBERT TRENT JONES, renowned American golf course architect, heard that club members were complaining because they considered he had made the short fourth hole at Baltusrol, New Jersey, too difficult while redesigning it for the 1954 U.S. Open. He had introduced an artificial water hazard that involved a long carry from tee to green. Trent Jones decided to silence his critics by volunteering to play the hole himself. He took an iron, placed the ball on the tee and struck it over the pond into the heart of the green. The ball broke right and went first bounce into the hole. 'Gentlemen,' said Trent Jones, 'I think that should settle all arguments.' He then strolled nonchantly back to the clubhouse.

Hendon professional **JOHN HUDSON** holed two consecutive holes-in-one in the 1971 Martini Tournament at Norwich. He aced the 195-yard eleventh and then the 311-yard downhill twelfth.

ROBERT MITRA achieved an astonishing hole-in-one at the tenth hole on the Miracle Hills golf course in Nebraska on 7 October 1965. From tee to green the hole is 408 metres (447 yards) and Mitra's ball was carried by a sudden gust of wind. It's the longest straight hole-in-one on record.

NORMAN MANLEY, an amateur from Long Beach, California, and **HARRY LEE BONNER** are the undisputed 'Ace-in-the-Hole' kings of golf. Bonner holed-in-one no fewer than fifty-seven times between 1967 and 1982. Manley has holed his tee shot forty-seven times and once aced successive par-fours at Del Valley, Saugus (330 yards and 290 yards) in 1964.

ART WALL, 1959 U.S. Masters champion, is the tee-time king among the professionals. He has holed-in-one forty-two times since he joined the professional Tour back in 1949.

Dr **JOSEPH BOYDSTONE** holed-in-one at the third, fourth and ninth holes during a round at Bakersfield, California, in 1962. He had eight other aces during that year.

CORBY ORR, of Littleton, Colorado, holed-in-one at the 103-yard fifth at the Riverside Golf Course, San Antonio, in 1975. What made it so remarkable is that Corby was just five years old!

HARK WHO'S TALKING

A collection of quotable quotes from a galaxy of golf stars

'If I wasn't a professional golfer you wouldn't catch me playing the game if they paid me.' — **CHRISTY O'CONNOR** during a round in Dublin played in a rainstorm

'Me retire? Retire to what? All I do now is fish and play golf.' — **JULIUS BOROS** on the subject of retirement

'It's a big advantage to be left-handed. Nobody knows enough about your swing to be able to mess you up with advice.' — **BOB CHARLES** when counting his blessings

'I learn English from American pros. That's why I speak so bad. I call it PGA English.' — **ROBERTO DE VICENZO**, apologizing for his fractured English

'The guys I'll never understand are the self-confessed non-competitors — the golfers who pick up $100,000-plus a year without ever winning a tournament and go around telling the world how happy they are to finish ninth every week.' — **JACK NICKLAUS**, talking about the will to win

'I hate to lose at anything, even at checkers, chess, pool — you name it. I feel if you ease up in any game it breeds a quitting attitude.' — **TOM WATSON**, talking about the will to win

'I once shot a wild, charging elephant in Africa and it kept coming at me until dropping to the ground at my feet. I wasn't a bit scared. It takes a four-foot putt to scare me to death.' — **SAM SNEAD**, on the pressures of golf

'Never hurry, never worry and be sure to smell the flowers along the way.' — **WALTER HAGEN,** the golfing showman who said he didn't want to be a millionaire but just wanted to live like one

'There's more tension in golf than in boxing because golfers bring it on themselves. It's silly really because it's not as if the golf ball is going to jump up and belt you on the whiskers, is it!' — **HENRY COOPER**, heavyweight boxing champion turned golf fanatic and famous for his hooking in the ring and off the tee

'I always travel first class. That way I *think* first class and I'm more likely to *play* first class.' — **RAY FLOYD** explaining how he gets through more than $50,000 a year in travelling expenses

120

'If you watch a game it's fun. If you play it, it's recreation. If you work at it, it's golf.' — **BOB HOPE** on his way into the rough to look for his ball

'I'm going to win so much this year that even my caddie will make it into the top twenty money-winners list.' — **LEE TREVINO**, in confident mood going into a new season

'Serenity is knowing that your worst shot is still going to be pretty good...The dollars aren't important – once you've got them.' — **JOHNNY MILLER**, in a philosophical mood

'If I put the ball where I can see it, I can't reach it. If I put it where I can reach it, I can't see it.' — **JACKIE GLEASON**, the rotund showbiz golfer when teeing off at a charity tournament

'I think those golfers who look as though they got dressed in the dark should be penalized two strokes each for offending the public eye.' — **DOUG SANDERS**, who prides himself on being the best-dressed golfer on the professional circuit

'I had a letter from this bloke in Scotland the other day. "Don't worry," he wrote. "It's not your fault. It's the ball's." He went on for ten pages explaining that no two golf balls had the same centre of gravity and that's why my putts veer away. So it's not me, gentlemen. It's the ball.' — **TONY JACKLIN**, giving a light-hearted explanation at a press conference for his lean spell following his British and U.S. Open triumphs

'If you're going to throw a club in temper, it's important to throw it ahead of you in the direction of the green. That way you don't waste energy going back to pick it up.' — **TOMMY BOLT**, who was once so notorious for his club-throwing tantrums that he was nicknamed 'Thunder Bolt'

'Maybe I should go to a sports shop and buy a trophy. That's the only way I'm going to get one.' — **SEVERIANO BALLESTEROS**, talking at St Andrews on the eve of the 1984 Open which, of course, he won

'If you think of yourself as an unlucky golfer, if you're sure you'll get a bad bounce, if you think you'll land in the water then you *will* be unlucky and get the bad bounce and land in the water. What you think, you will be.' — **GARY PLAYER** on the power of positive thinking that has helped lift him into the land of golfing legend

'Oh well, no matter what happens I can always dig ditches for a living.' — **ARNOLD PALMER**, talking during a rare losing run

GOLFING GREATS WHO CONQUERED THEIR HANDICAPS

TOMMY ARMOUR lost the sight of one eye during the First World War but went on to win every major championship. As an amateur, Edinburgh-born Armour played for Britain against the United States and as a professional for the U.S. against Britain. He was a meticulous player who would sometimes waggle his club more than twenty times before launching into a shot. Armour, the 'Silver Scot' who later became acknowledged as the world's leading golf teacher, was a stickler for the rules. He once saw an opponent craftily teeing a ball up in the rough. Armour quietly walked over, trod the ball firmly into the ground with his spiked heel and said: 'That's where it landed and that's where you play it.'

BYRON NELSON, a Texan who quickly established himself as one of the world's greatest golfers after turning professional in 1932, was exempted from military service because he was a haemophiliac.

GAY BREWER, winner of the U.S. Masters in 1967, broke his elbow at the age of seven when playing American football. He took up golf to get full movement back into his arm and this accounted for one of the oddest swings ever seen on the pro circuit. He himself described the path of the clubhead as 'a sort of figure eight'.

ED FURGOL became 1954 U.S. Open champion despite a childhood accident that left him with a withered left arm which was bent at the elbow and eight inches shorter than his right.

BILLY CASPER, U.S. Open champion in 1959 and 1966 and Masters champion in 1970, went on a diet of buffalo meat to combat a recurring allergy problem. It must have worked because he became the second player to win more than a million dollars in prize money.

GENE LITTLER, U.S. Open champion in 1961, underwent major surgery for cancer in 1969. He returned to the U.S. circuit to challenge for the major titles and was runner up in the U.S. PGA championship in 1977 at the age of forty-seven.

DOUGLAS BADER, the RAF hero who continued to reach for the sky despite losing both legs while on wartime flying missions, was the man who gave most encouragement to disabled golfers by stomping around countless courses on his tin legs and recording respectable scores.

ROY CASTLE
How I Would Like To Play the Game

I would consider myself the perfect golfer if I could have...

The **DRIVE** of **FERRARI**
The **SWING** of **COUNT BASIE**
The **LONG IRONS** game of **ROBERT WADLOW** (8 ft 6 in. tall)
The **SHORT IRONS** game of **RONNIE CORBETT**
The **BUNKER SHOTS** of **THE EIGHTH ARMY**
The **PUTTING** of **GEOFF CAPES**
The **TEMPERAMENT** of **JOB**

'With this combination I would be unbeatable on the golf course. The only problem I would have is getting a caddie because I would want to be carried as well as my golf clubs.'

ROY CASTLE is one of Britain's most versatile and popular entertainers who has been enjoying a smash-hit success with Tommy Steele at the London Palladium in *Singin' in the Rain*. Although you wouldn't think it to look at his identikit of the perfect golfer, he treats his golf with deadly seriousness. In fact he could star in a new show at the Palladium: *Swingin' in the Rain*!

THE TEXAS GOLF BARONS v THE CALIFORNIAN KINGS

Texans and Californians like to boast that their state produces the greatest golfers. Judge for yourself from this 'Dashing Dozen' list:

CHARLES COODY Stamford	**GEORGE ARCHER** San Francisco
BEN CRENSHAW Austin	**BILLY CASPER** San Diego
JIMMY DEMARET Houston	**OLIN DUTRA** Monterey
LEE ELDER Dallas	**AL GEIBERGER** Red Bluff
RALPH GULDAHL Dallas	**TONY LEMA** Oakland
BEN HOGAN Nelson	**GENE LITTLER** San Diego
DON JANUARY Plainview	**JOHNNY MILLER** San Francisco
TOM KITE Austin	**PHIL RODGERS** San Diego
LLOYD MANGRUM Trenton	**BOB ROSBURG** San Francisco
BYRON NELSON Fort Worth	**CRAIG STADLER** San Diego
BILL ROGERS Waco	**DAVE STOCKTON** San Bernardino
LEE TREVINO Dallas	**KEN VENTURI** San Francisco

CADDIES WHO BECAME KINGS

These are among the many players who started out carrying clubs before swinging their way to success.

HARRY VARDON (*Great Britain*)
WALTER HAGEN (*USA*)
BEN HOGAN (*USA*)
BYRON NELSON (*USA*)
GENE SARAZEN (*USA*)
SAM SNEAD (*USA*)
DOUG SANDERS (*USA*)
NORMAN VON NIDA (*Australia*)
TOM KIDD (*Great Britain*)
ROBERTO DE VICENZO (*Argentina*)*
SEVE BALLESTEROS (*Spain*)
TONY LEMA (*USA*)
TONY JACKLIN (*Great Britain*)
JUAN RODRIGUEZ (*Puerto Rico*)
BERNHARD LANGER (*West Germany*)
ROBERT FERGUSON (*Great Britain*)
HASSAN HASSANEIN (*Egypt*)
JEAN GARAIALDE (*France*)

*Roberto was promoted to caddie after working as a 'pond boy', retrieving wayward balls from ponds and impossible lies.

THE NAME GAME

Nicknames of thirty star golfers...

THE SILVER SCOT (Tommy Armour)
THE GOLDEN BEAR (Jack Nicklaus)
THE WALRUS (Craig Stadler)
CHAMPAGNE TONY (Tony Lema)
THE IRON MAN (Bruce Crampton)
THE HAIG (Walter Hagen)
THE SQUIRE (Gene Sarazen)
THE MAESTRO (Henry Cotton)
THE HORSE (Harold Henning)
THE WEE ICE MON (Ben Hogan)
TOY BULLDOG (Brian Huggett)
OLD MUFFIN FACE (Bobby Locke)
LORD BYRON (Byron Nelson)
WRISTY CHRISTY (Christy O'Connor Snr)
SLAMMIN' SAM (Sam Snead)
THE JOPLIN GHOST (Horton Smith)
LIGHT HORSE (Harry Cooper)
THE MIGHTY MITE (Bob Toski)
LITTLE POISON (Paul Runyan)
MUSCLES (Frank Stranahan)
SUPERMEX (Lee Trevino)
BUFFALO BILL (Billy Casper)
MR LU (Liang Huan Lu)
THE GREAT WHITE SHARK (Greg Norman)
THE WALKING ONE IRON (Ken Brown)
MR CONSISTENCY (Miller Barber)
THE TOWERING INFERNO (Tom Weiskopf)
THE MOOSE (Julius Boros)
GENE THE MACHINE (Gene Littler)
PRETTY BOY (Raymond Floyd)

Lee Trevino...Supermex and a Superstar

ERIC SYKES
How I Would Like To Play the Game

I would consider myself the perfect golfer if I could have...

The **DRIVE** of **SEVE BALLESTEROS**
The **SWING** of **SAM SNEAD**
The **LONG IRONS** game of **ARNOLD PALMER**
The **SHORT IRONS** game of **SEVE BALLESTEROS**
The **BUNKER SHOTS** of **GARY PLAYER**
The **PUTTING** of **TOM WATSON**
The **TEMPERAMENT** of **JACK NICKLAUS**

'Having all these qualities at my age would make me a freak on the golf course. I reckon Tom Watson is the closest thing there has been to perfection, but I would fancy my chances against him if I could just knock about twenty-five strokes off my average score.'

ERIC SYKES is not only one of Britain's best-loved comedy actors but also a talented scriptwriter. During a long, fanatical and sometimes frustrating love affair with golf he has managed to get his handicap down to fifteen. He is a regular on the charity-tournament circuit.

SECTION FIVE
JUST AMAZING!

A mixed golf bag of amazing facts and deeds:

JOHNNY MILLER picked up the richest pot in history at Sun City, Bophuthatswana, on 3 January 1982, when he beat Seve Ballesteros at the ninth extra hole of a sudden-death play-off for the record $500,000 first prize. Seve's consolation was a prize of $160,000.

During the 1945 season, **BYRON NELSON** had one of the greatest winning streaks on record. He won eleven consecutive PGA Open tournaments, and in all that year won seventeen titles. He shot nineteen rounds in a row under 70 and compiled a stroke average of 68.33. In 113 consecutive tournaments he was never once out of the money.

ROBERTO DE VICENZO robbed himself of the chance of winning the U.S. Masters at Augusta in 1968. In the final round U.S. Ryder Cup player Tommy Aaron, with whom he was paired, marked a four on de Vicenzo's card after the seventeenth hole when millions of television viewers and the course spectators had seen him sink his putt for a three. His actual finishing score for the round was 65 which would have taken him into a play-off for the title with the American Bob Goalby. But de Vicenzo signed the card without double checking and as it showed a return of 66 that was the score that, according to the rules, had to be recorded. The big, amiable Argentinian shrugged at the presentation ceremony and said in fractured English: 'What a stupid I am.'

There was a sensational climax to the *News of the World* Match Play championship semi-final between defending champion Brian Huggett and his fellow Welshman Dai Rees. Huggett was one up standing on the eighteenth tee but lost the hole without playing a stroke. A wildly hooked drive by Rees struck a post and rebounded against Huggett's golf bag. The law states that 'if a player's ball be stopped or deflected by his opponent, his caddie or equipment, the opponent's side shall lose the hole'. So Huggett had to forfeit the hole and, to rub it in, Rees then went on to win the nineteenth hole and the match.

LLOYD MANGRUM, U.S. Open champion in 1946, was penalized two strokes for blowing an insect off his ball during a play-off for the championship in 1950.

The longest hole in the world is the seventh at the Sano Course, Satsuki, in Japan. It runs 831 metres (909 yards) from tee to green and is a par seven. The sixth hole at Koolan Island Golf Course, Western Australia, measures 782 metres (860) yards and is also a par seven.

Spectators gathered round the fifth green at the U.S. National Seniors' Open at the Winterwood Course, Las Vegas, wondered who had hit his second shot through the green on the 450-yard hole. They could not see anybody on the fairway. The ball had been driven from the tee by sixty-four-year-old Los Angeles professional **MIKE AUSTIN**. Aided by a 35mph tailwind, the ball had travelled sixty-five yards past the flag for a drive of 515 yards.

The longest recorded drive on the U.S. tournament circuit is 426 yards by **GEORGE BAYER** in the 1955 Tucson Open. Bayer was famed for his big hitting and once cleared 500 yards with a drive that put him within chipping distance of a 589-yard hole in Australia.

CRAIG WOOD, U.S. Masters champion in 1941, hit an extraordinary drive in his play-off for the 1933 British Open with fellow-American Densmore Shute. Playing the 530-yard fifth at St Andrews, he drove into a bunker guarding the green. His wind-assisted shot was measured at 430 yards. Wood was beaten by five strokes in the thirty-six-hole play-off.

LEW WORSHAM, 1947 U.S. Open champion, holed a 135-yard wedge shot for an eagle two at the 410-yard final hole of the Tam O'Shanter 'World Championship' at Chicago in 1953. It gave him victory by one stroke and a $25,000 first prize.

BILLY CASPER sank his second shot on the 580-yards fourteenth hole at Crans-sur-Sierre for an albatross (three under par) in the 1971 Swiss Open.

JOHNNY MILLER holed out his second shot with a three-wood on the 558-yard fifth hole in the 1972 Open at Muirfield. He produced this spectacular albatross on his way to a round of 66.

HARRY BRADSHAW drove into the rough at the fifth hole in the second round of the 1949 Open at Sandwich. He found his ball lodged against the neck of a broken beer bottle. The Irishman risked disqualification if he claimed the ball was unplayable and so elected to play it as it lay. He took out his sandblaster and smashed though the glass to send the ball thirty yards towards the hole. Bradshaw got down in six on the par-four hole and at the end of the final round was tied for the lead with eventual champion Bobby Locke.

Billy Casper...down in two at a 580-yard hole

BOBBY JONES holed a monster putt of around 100 feet (30 metres) for a birdie three on the Hole o' Cross fifth at St Andrews on his way to a first round 68 that set him up for his second Open championship. The longest officially recorded putt in a major tournament was **CARY MIDDLECOFF'S** effort of 86 feet (26 metres) on the thirteenth green in the U.S. Masters at Augusta in 1955.

ROBERT GARDNER, U.S. Amateur golf champion in 1909 and 1915, was also the world pole vault record holder. A Yale University student, he cleared 13 feet 1 inch in 1912. He was invited to represent the United States in the 1912 Stockholm Olympics but declined because he preferred to concentrate on his golf.

Scottish golfer **ERIC BROWN** had a peerless record in the Ryder Cup. On each of the four occasions he played he won his singles match and in 1969 he was non-playing captain of the British side that figured in the only tie in the history of the competition. His American 'victims' in the Ryder Cup singles were Lloyd Mangrum (1953, victory by two holes), Jerry Barber (1955, three and two), Tommy Bolt (1957, four and three) and Cary Middlecoff (1959, four and three).

H.H. (HAROLD HORSFALL) HILTON was one of the greatest personalities in the history of British amateur golf. He held the unique record of winning the British Open twice (1892 and 1897), the British Amateur title four times (1900, 1901, 1911 and 1913) and the United States Amateur championship in 1911 at the age of forty-two. He later became an outstanding teacher and a respected journalist who edited *Golf Illustrated* and *Golf Monthly*.

JACK ALLAN, a medical student, rolled up at Muirfield for the 1897 British Amateur championship on a bicycle and amazed spectators by going on to the course wearing the clothes and shoes in which he had arrived. Even more amazing was the standard of his golf. Competing in his first championship after less than five years playing the game, he won the title by beating the highly-rated James Robb in the final. Allan, alas, died the following year shortly after qualifying as a doctor.

PETER ALLISS, one of the most gifted British golfers of all time and now the respected 'Voice of Golf' on television, worked hard as captain of the Professional Golfers' Association in 1962 to remove the cloth-cap image of club professionals. He illustrated the point with a story about his purple patch in 1958 when he won the Spanish, Portuguese and Italian Open titles within a month. Peter returned triumphant to his Parkstone Club, only to be greeted by an irate member who growled: 'Where have you been? I've been waiting three weeks for a lesson.'

132

There have been many instances of golfers being disqualified for arriving late at the tee but **JOHNNY BULLA** went one better in the 1941 U.S. Open. Bulla, the Virginian who played out of Chicago and was twice runner-up in the British Open, suffered the embarrassment of being disqualified for teeing off *before* his time.

JOHNNY McDERMOTT, the first American-born winner of the U.S. Open in 1911, set sail from New York to challenge for the British Open at Prestwick in 1914. He had got his dates mixed up and arrived a day too late to compete in the qualifying rounds.

TOMMY BOLT, U.S. Open champion in 1958, had a violent temper that earned him the nickname 'Thunder Bolt'. One of his most publicized outbursts came in the U.S. Open at Denver in 1960 when he mishit a shot into a pond at the twelfth. He had a heated argument with a U.S. GA official as to where he should place the ball for his penalty shot and this so upset his concentration that he three-putted the next hole, bogeyed the next and hooked two drives into the lake off the eighteenth tee. By now Bolt was in his most thunderous mood and at the end of the round he swung his driver around his head and sent it spinning into the lake. A small boy came racing out of the crowd, dived into the lake and came out triumphantly holding the driver. Bolt's caddie walked forward to receive it but, to the cheers of the gallery, the boy side-stepped him and raced off into the distance clutching his prize.

BOB GOALBY, the 1968 Masters champion, is another golfer who has an explosive temper. He once dived into a water hazard in rage, and on another occasion angrily kicked his way through puddles on a fairway after hooking a shot. In the 1968 Los Angeles Open he became so frustrated with the slow play of his partners that he forged on ahead and finished the round on his own. An Italian professional became so infuriated with his procession of loose shots in the 1968 French Open that he threw first his ball and then his club over an out-of-bounds fence and then jumped over it himself and quit the tournament.

Airshots are the most frustrating of all ways to concede strokes. It is doubly agonizing when it happens on the green. **ANDREW KIRKALDY**, runner-up three times in the British Open and third on three other occasions, watched his pitch to the fourteenth green in the 1889 Open at Musselburgh stop just an inch short of the hole. When he arrived at the green he took a casual one-handed swing at the ball and missed. It was a slip that cost him the championship. Willie Park Jnr forced a play-off that he won by five shots.

LEO DIEGEL, U.S. PGA winner in 1928 and 1929 but more famous for being a runner-up than a champion, faced a simple putt on the eighteenth green that would have taken him into a play-off for the British Open championship at St Andrews in 1933. He bent over the ball in his curious elbows-at-right-angles style — it became known as 'diegeling' — and after several seconds of hard concentration pushed the putter head forward and missed the ball completely.

HALE IRWIN, usually the most meticulous of all golfers, had a simple tap-in putt of two inches on the fourteenth green in the third round of the 1983 Open at Royal Birkdale. He attempted to play it with the back of his putter and missed. The next day he was one stroke off forcing a tie with Tom Watson.

AL GEIBERGER holds the record for the lowest score over eighteen holes in a major tournament on the United States circuit. He scored 59 in the second round of the Danny Thomas Classic in Memphis in 1977. Geiberger started on the tenth tee and completed the half in 30, coming home in 29. He had six pars, eleven birdies and an eagle. He sank an eight-foot putt on the final green to break the '60' barrier. Seven Americans recorded scores of 60 in major tournaments during the 1950s — **AL BORSCH** (Texas Open, 1951). **BILL NARY** (El Paso Open, 1952), **TED KROLL** (Texas Open, 1954), **TOMMY BOLT** (Insurance City Open, 1954), **MIKE SOUCHAK** (Texas Open, 1955) and **SAM SNEAD** (Dallas Open, 1957).

SAM SNEAD (White Sulphur Springs, 1959), **GARY PLAYER** (Brazilian Open in Rio, 1974) and Britain's **DAVID JAGGER** (Pro-Am tournament in Nigeria, 1973) have returned rounds of 59 in non-PGA tournaments.

NIGEL DENHAM must have felt in need of a stiff drink when he saw where his ball had come to rest at the eighteenth at Moortown during the 1974 English Open Amateur Stroke Play championship. He overhit his second shot to the green and the ball bounced up the clubhouse steps, through the open door and ricochetted off a wall into the club bar. As the clubhouse was not out of bounds Denham decided to try to play the ball back to the green. He opened the bar-room window and pitched the ball back on to the green and to within three yards of the flag. It was later ruled by the R&A that he should have been penalized two strokes for opening the window because the clubhouse was an immoveable object and therefore, said the R&A, no part of it should have been moved.

BOBBY LOCKE struck what looked a perfect tee-shot at the short 100-yard twelfth hole in the 1936 Irish Open at Dublin but when he got to the green was unable to find his ball. His caddie removed the pin to look in the hole and the ball was discovered trapped in

Arnold Palmer...really rooted for the Open championship

the furled flag. It dropped to within inches of the hole and Locke sank his putt for a birdie two.

BOBBY JONES uncharacteristically drew his drive at the seventeenth in the final round of the 1926 Open at Royal Lytham and the ball came to rest in a shallow bunker 170 yards from the green. His fellow-American Al Watrous, with whom he was locked in a neck-and-neck duel for the championship, was on the green in two. Jones took his mashie iron (equivalent of a four-iron) and struck a glorious shot to the heart of the green. He got down in four while Watrous three-putted for a five. Jones went on to win his first British Open and that remarkable shot from the bunker has been commemorated by a bronze plaque at the spot where he played the ball.

ARNOLD PALMER removed a bush — roots and all — from the ground with a mighty six-iron shot at the sixteenth on the final round of the 1961 Open at Royal Birkdale. He had pushed his drive into heavy rough and found his ball in an almost unplayable position beneath the small bush. To most golfers it would have been a case of trying to play the ball out on to the fairway but the one and only Palmer decided to go for the green 140 yards away. He dug the ball — and the bush — out with a prodigious shot. The ball landed on the green and he two-putted for his par on the way to the first of his two successive Open championships. The bush was never replanted and in it's place there is a plaque that reads simply: ARNOLD PALMER, THE OPEN CHAMPIONSHIP 1961.

Three years later in the Australian Wills Masters tournament in Melbourne, **ARNOLD PALMER** played yet another extraordinary shot. He hooked his second shot at the ninth hole high into the fork of a gum tree. Palmer clambered up the twenty feet to where his ball lay and, using his No. 1 iron hammer-style, knocked it forward thirty yards from where he chipped on to the green and one-putted.

SEWSUNKER SEWGOLUM, born in Durban of Indian parentage, was one of those rare golfers who tasted success with an unorthodox grip in which his left hand was positioned below his right. He was Dutch Open champion in 1959, 1960 and 1964.

JOHNNY BULLA, runner-up in the British Open in 1939 and 1946, played right-handed from tee to green and then used to putt on his left side.

GARDNER DICKINSON held Ben Hogan in such great reverence that he once flew 6,000 miles for a lesson from his idol. Like Hogan, Dickinson wore a white cloth cap and his fellow-pros swore he even copied Hogan's post-accident limp!

RAY FLOYD, famed for leading a swinging existence on and off the course, had an interesting job away from the golf tour. He managed 'The Ladybirds', the first topless nightclub band.

HENRY RANSOM, a Texan whose career bridged Second World War, was having a tough time in a tournament at Cypress Point. He struggled at the notorious sixteenth when he put his ball on to the Pacific Beach. Henry took his wedge and smacked the ball towards the green. It hit the lip of a bunker and rebounded into his stomach. He threw his club to the ground and said: 'That's it! When a hole starts hitting back, I quit.'

ARCHIE COMPSTON, one of Britain's most accomplished golfers between the wars, earned himself a permanent place in golfing legend when he beat the great Walter Hagen by the atonishing margin of eighteen and seventeen in a challenge match at Moor Park in 1928. A week later in the Open at Sandwich Hagen got his revenge when he won the championship with Compston in third place. One particular victory made Compston popular throughout the country. It was against the taxman. He was known to have made a lot of money from backing himself in private challenge matches against rich amateurs. The Inland Revenue tried to tax him on his winnings but he beat them in court. Compston coached the Prince of Wales before he became Edward Vlll and once accompanied him on a cruise during which 3,000 balls were hit from a tee on the deck into the Mediterranean.

BOBBY JONES went back to his hotel for lunch during the break before his final round in the Open at Royal Lytham in 1926. On his return to the course the gateman did not recognize him and refused to let him in. Rather than protest, 'Gentleman' Bobby paid his entrance money and proceeded to the first tee to start the round in which he clinched his first Open championship.

On his way to his historic Grand Slam in 1930 Bobby Jones hit what became known as the 'Miracle Shot of Golf'. He was playing the ninth hole in the U.S. Open at Interlachen when he struck a shot across a lake that spellbound spectators swore skidded across the water before emerging safe on the other side. What actually happened is that the ball bounced off a lilypad that saved it from a watery grave that just might have sunk the 'Grand Slam'. It seems that 'The Master's' followers were only disappointed that he didn't walk across the water after his ball.

KY LAFFOON, a part Red Indian golf professional from Zinc, Arkansas, was one of the great eccentrics of the U.S. Tour during the 1930s and 1940s. He was particularly abusive towards his clubs if they did not produce the shots he required. During one eventful round his putter was less than cooperative. He tried bending it over

Ray Floyd...a swinger on and off the course

his knee. That failed. Then he tossed into a lake but retrieved it for 'one more chance'. When it let him down on the final green he pronounced a sentence of hard labour. He tied the unfortunate putter with a piece of string to the bumper of his car and dragged it all the way home.

WALTER DANECKI, a forty-three-year-old self-described 'golf professional' from Milwaukee, astonished everybody in the second qualifying round for the 1965 Open at Royal Birkdale when he recorded an amazing score of 58. What made it so amazing was that it was his total for the first nine holes! He came back in 55 for an aggregate 113. His first round total was 108 and he missed the qualifying total of 151 by a mere 70 strokes. Walter later confessed that he was not really a professional − 'I just wanted to try to win that crock of gold.'

In the Open qualifying round of 1976 **MAURICE FLITCROFT** recorded an eighteen-holes total of 121. Six years later − describing himself as 'Gerald Hoppy, a professional from Switzer-land' − Maurice tried again but was persuaded to retire from the qualifying round after amassing 63 shots to the ninth hole. Maurice was, in fact, a crane-driver from Barrow-in-Furness.

Which has been the golf shot watched by the biggest television audience? If you're trying to think of a shot by Nicklaus, Watson or Ballesteros you're not aiming high enough. It was actually a six-iron shot struck by astronaut Alan Shephard while on the moon during the Apollo 14 expedition of 1971. The club is now a prized exhibit in the U.S. PGA Museum.

HENRY COOPER
How I Would Like To Play the Game

I would consider myself the perfect golfer if I could have...

The **DRIVE** of **JACK NICKLAUS**
The **SWING** of **SAM SNEAD**
The **LONG IRONS** game of **ARNOLD PALMER**
The **SHORT IRONS** game of **SEVE BALLESTEROS**
The **BUNKER SHOTS** of **GARY PLAYER**
The **PUTTING** of **BOB CHARLES**
The **TEMPERAMENT** of **LEE TREVINO**

'I'm a "leftie" so I've always closely followed Bob Charles, who is far and away the most successful left-handed golfer of all time. Mind you, my partners would tell you I play the game more like Ray Charles! Since I retired from boxing, golf has been my biggest passion. I would play every day of the week if time allowed.'

HENRY COOPER remains one of Britain's favourite sportsmen more than a dozen years after his retirement from the ring. In a distinguished boxing career he won a record three Lonsdale Belts outright, held the British, Commonwealth and European titles and fought Muhammad Ali for the world crown in 1966. He will long be remembered for the left hook that dropped Ali (then Cassius Clay) in a non-title fight in 1963. He was famed and feared for his left hook — 'Enery's 'Ammer — and unfortunately for him he has also got a hook that frequently wrecks his golfing scorecard! Henry works ceaselessly for charitable causes and never misses the chance to play in charity golf tournaments where his popularity is proved time and again by the massive galleries that he pulls.

SECTION SIX
ALL ABOUT THE OPEN

The British Open is officially known as 'The Open' simply because it was the first open golf championship in the world. This section deals with lists connected with the Open and we tee off with a public opinion poll that was carried out exclusively for *The Book of Golf Lists*.

THE GREAT OPEN OPINION POLL

One thousand* of the record gathering of 187,753 golf lovers who jammed the Old Course at St Andrews for the 1984 Open championship kindly gave us their views on a variety of issues connected with the oldest of the great championships:

WHO HAS BEEN THE GREATEST OPEN CHAMPION OF THE LAST THIRTY YEARS?

1	JACK NICKLAUS *(USA)*	39%
2	ARNOLD PALMER *(USA)*	23%
3	TOM WATSON *(USA)*	17%
4	GARY PLAYER *(South Africa)*	7%
5	LEE TREVINO *(USA)*	5%
5	PETER THOMSON *(Australia)*	4%
6	SEVE BALLESTEROS *(Spain)*	3%
	Others	2%

WHO HAS BEEN THE GREATEST BRITISH PLAYER IN THE OPEN IN THE PAST THIRTY YEARS?

1	TONY JACKLIN	76%
2	DAI REES	7%
3	DAVE THOMAS	5%
4	ERIC BROWN	4%
4	NEIL COLES	3%
5	PETER OOSTERHUIS	2%
	Others	3%

*1,024 people were interviewed at St Andrews during the Open in July, 1984.

141

WHO HAS BEEN THE GREATEST POST-WAR PLAYER NEVER TO HAVE WON THE OPEN?

1	BILLY CASPER *(USA)*	17%
2	RAYMOND FLOYD *(USA)*	15%
3	DAI REES *(GB)*	13%
4	GREG NORMAN *(Australia)*	11%
5	HALE IRWIN *(USA)*	9%
6	DOUG SANDERS *(USA)*	8%
7	PETER OOSTERHUIS *(GB)*	6%
8	BEN CRENSHAW *(USA)*	5%
9	NICK FALDO *(GB)*	4%
10	SANDY LYLE *(GB)*	3%
	Others	9%

WHO DO YOU CONSIDER THE MOST EXCITING AND ENTERTAINING OF TODAY'S TOP PLAYERS?

1	SEVE BALLESTEROS *(Spain)*	36%
2	JACK NICKLAUS *(USA)*	19%
3	GREG NORMAN *(Australia)*	14%
4	LEE TREVINO *(USA)*	9%
5	JOHNNY MILLER *(USA)*	7%
6	TOM WATSON *(USA)*	6%
7	BERNHARD LANGER *(Germany)*	3%
	Others	6%

WHICH MODERN PLAYER HAS DONE MOST TO PROMOTE THE GOOD IMAGE OF GOLF?

1	JACK NICKLAUS *(USA)*	42%
2	TOM WATSON *(USA)*	21%
3	SEVE BALLESTEROS *(Spain)*	13%
4	GARY PLAYER *(South Africa)*	9%
5	JOHNNY MILLER *(USA)*	7%
5	LEE TREVINO *(USA)*	6%
	Others	2%

WHO IS YOUR CURRENT FAVOURITE GOLFER OUTSIDE THE USA AND BRITAIN?

1	SEVE BALLESTEROS *(Spain)*	59%
2	GARY PLAYER *(South Africa)*	16%
3	GREG NORMAN *(Australia)*	11%
4	BERNHARD LANGER *(Germany)*	7%
5	ISAO AOKI *(Japan)*	4%
	Others	3%

WHICH TWO PLAYERS WOULD YOU PIT AGAINST EACH OTHER IN A 'DREAM MATCH' IF YOU COULD PICK FROM ANY ERA?

This question produced scores of different combinations. Among the most popular pairings which would have graced any course were:

JACK NICKLAUS	v	BOBBY JONES
ARNOLD PALMER	v	WALTER HAGEN
HENRY COTTON	v	SEVE BALLESTEROS
BEN HOGAN	v	TOM WATSON
SAM SNEAD	v	GARY PLAYER
HARRY VARDON	v	LEE TREVINO

WHICH PLAYER HAS ACHIEVED MOST FOR BRITISH GOLF DURING THE PAST FIFTY YEARS?

1	HENRY COTTON	51%
2	TONY JACKLIN	46%
	Others	3%

Henry Cotton...'The Maestro' of British golf

DO YOU CONSIDER THE PRIZE MONEY IN MODERN GOLF TOO HIGH?

TOO HIGH	34%
SHOULD BE HIGHER	22%
ABOUT RIGHT	44%

IF YOU COULD PUT TOGETHER THE 'PERFECT PLAYER' WHOSE SHOTS WOULD HE HAVE?*

The DRIVE of Jack Nicklaus	51%
The SWING of Sam Snead	61%
The LONG IRON shots of Seve Ballesteros	42%
The SHORT GAME of Tom Watson	39%
The SAND SHOTS of Lee Trevino	29%
The PUTTING of Bobby Locke	27%
The TEMPERAMENT of Gary Player	31%

THE GOLFER WHO HAS COME NEAREST TO BEING THE PERFECT PLAYER?

1	JACK NICKLAUS (USA)	42%
2	TOM WATSON (USA)	17%
3	ARNOLD PALMER (USA)	12%
4	BOBBY JONES (USA)	9%
5	BEN HOGAN (USA)	6%
6	GARY PLAYER (South Africa)	4%
7	LEE TREVINO (USA)	3%
	Others	7%

*We give the player who polled most votes in each category.

THE OPEN COURSES

The British Open championship has been staged on fourteen courses since it was first contested at Prestwick back in 1860:

PRESTWICK
1860—72 inclusive, 1875, 1878, 1881, 1884, 1887, 1890, 1893, 1898, 1903, 1908, 1914, 1925
ST ANDREWS
1873, 1876, 1879, 1882, 1885, 1888, 1891, 1895, 1900, 1905, 1910, 1921, 1927, 1933, 1939, 1946, 1955, 1957, 1960, 1964, 1970, 1978, 1984
MUSSELBURGH
1874, 1877, 1880, 1883, 1886, 1889
MUIRFIELD
1892, 1896, 1901, 1906, 1912, 1929, 1935, 1948, 1959, 1966, 1972, 1980
ROYAL ST GEORGE'S, SANDWICH
1894, 1899, 1904, 1911, 1922, 1928, 1934, 1938, 1949, 1981,1985
PRINCE'S, SANDWICH
1932
HOYLAKE
1897, 1902, 1907, 1913, 1924, 1930, 1936, 1947, 1956, 1967
DEAL
1909, 1920
ROYAL TROON
1923, 1950, 1962, 1973, 1982
ROYAL LYTHAM
1926, 1952, 1958, 1963, 1969, 1974, 1979
CARNOUSTIE
1931, 1937, 1953, 1968, 1975
ROYAL PORTRUSH
1951
ROYAL BIRKDALE
1954, 1961, 1965, 1971, 1976, 1983
TURNBERRY
1977

CHAMPIONS AGAIN AND AGAIN

These are the golfers who have been winners of the Open on more than one occasion:

6: HARRY VARDON
(Great Britain)
1896−98−99−1903−11−14

5: JAMES BRAID
(Great Britain)
1901−05−06−08−10

5: J.H. TAYLOR
(Great Britain)
1894−95−1900−09−13

5: PETER THOMSON
(Australia)
1954−55−56−58−65

5: TOM WATSON
(USA)
1975−77−80−82−83

4: WILLIE PARK Snr
(Great Britain)
1860−63−66−75

4: TOM MORRIS Snr
(Great Britain)
1861−62−64−67

4: TOM MORRIS Jnr
(Great Britain)
1868−69−70−72

4: WALTER HAGEN
(USA)
1922−24−28−29

4: BOBBY LOCKE
(South Africa)
1949−50−52−57

3: JAMIE ANDERSON
(Great Britain)
1877−78−79

3: BOB FERGUSON
(Great Britain)
1880−81−82

3: BOBBY JONES
(USA)
1926−27−30

3: HENRY COTTON
(Great Britain)
1934−37−48

3: GARY PLAYER
(South Africa)
1959−68−74

3: JACK NICKLAUS
(USA)
1966−70−78

2: BOB MARTIN
(Great Britain)
1876−85

2: WILLIE PARK Jnr
(Great Britain)
1887−89

2: HAROLD HILTON
(Great Britain)
1892−97

2: ARNOLD PALMER
(USA)
1961−62

2: LEE TREVINO
(USA)
1971−72

2: SEVE BALLESTEROS
(Spain)
1979−84

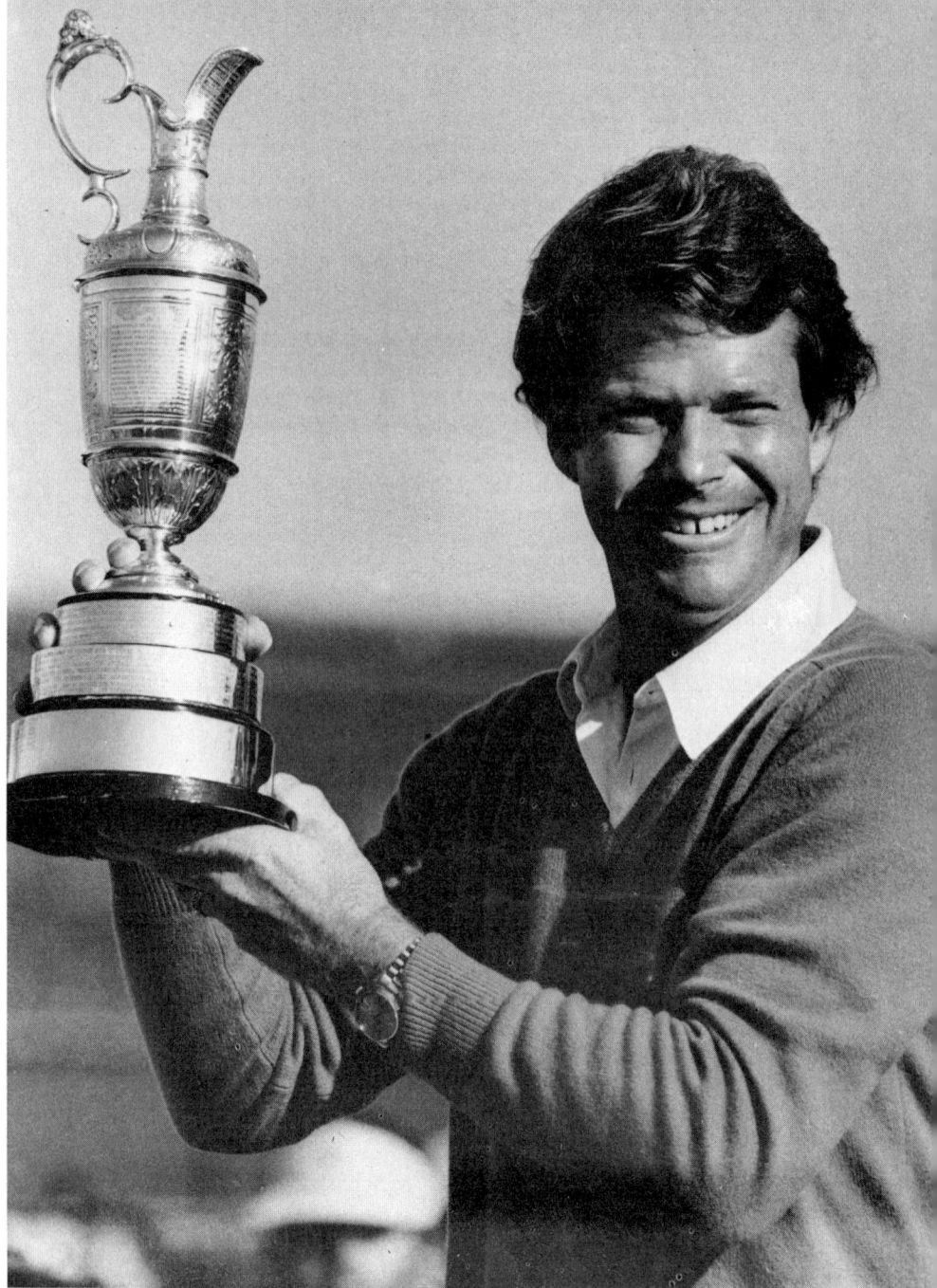

Tom Watson...five times winner of the British Open

THE GREAT TRIUMVIRATE

No reference to the British Open would be complete without mention of the trio of 'Golden Age' champions who became known collectively as 'The Great Triumvirate'.

JAMES BRAID was, along with J.H. Taylor and Harry Vardon, one of the 'Big Three' who dominated British golf at the turn of the century. Born in Elie, Fifeshire, in 1870, he first emerged as a potential champion while working in London as a clubmaker at the Army and Navy Stores. He used to play in exhibition matches during his one afternoon off a week and, following a halved match with J.H. Taylor, he set off on a professional career that lifted him into the land of golfing legend. He won the Open championship five times between 1901 and 1910 and was still good enough at the age of fifty-seven to reach the final of the British Match Play championship that he had won four times during his peak years. He became a highly-regarded course architect, was a founder member of the Professional Golfers' Association, and was the professional at Walton Heath for a span of forty-five years during which he commanded great respect and affection. His calm temperament was best displayed during the 1908 Open at Prestwick when he took a disastrous eight at the notorious 'Cardinal' hole in the third round. It would have destroyed the concentration and fluency of most players but he kept his head and went on to win with what was then a record aggregate of 291.

J.H. TAYLOR was the first of the 'Great Triumvirate' to win the British Open championship in 1894. It was the first of five wins (also 1895, 1900, 1909 and 1913). He was famed for his uncanny accuracy regardless of the course or the conditions, as he proved in the 1913 Open at Hoylake when he remained in command despite gale-force winds that were blowing his opponents out of contention. Though lacking the great power of Braid and the grace of Vardon, Taylor was a master of iron play and his putting was exceptional. He played in the first match between Great Britain and the United States in 1921 and was a winning captain of the Ryder Cup team eighteen years later. Taylor was still good enough at the age of fifty-three to lead Walter Hagen after two rounds of the 1925 Open in which he finally finished fifth.

The founder in 1902 of the Professional Golfers' Association, he became the Grand Old Man of Golf who lived until he was ninety-one. In 1949 he was made an honorary member of the Royal and Ancient. He spent his last years close to the Westward Ho! Club where he had started work as a boy, and of which he was made president in 1957.

HARRY VARDON won the British Open championship a record six times between 1896 and 1914 and had a major worldwide influence on the game. He started to play while a caddie at Grouville in the Channel Islands where he was born in 1870. In 1900 he toured the United States and helped popularize the sport. The highlight of his visit was victory in the U.S. Open, with his great friend and rival J.H. Taylor in second place. He was beaten in a play-off for the U.S. Open by Francis Ouimet in 1913 and seven years later, at the age of fifty, he finished equal second in the U.S. Open just a stroke behind his fellow-Briton Ted Ray.

Vardon was master of every aspect of the game, although in the second half of his career he became an unpredictable and at times abysmal putter. His name lives on in golf in the 'Vardon grip' and also with two trophies — one in Britain and one in the United States — that carry his name. Both the trophies are awarded to players with the lowest stroke average, which is fitting because few golfers have ever been able to match Vardon's accuracy from tee to green. The no doubt apocryphal story that has been handed down through generations of golfers is that Vardon could never play two rounds on the same day because his afternoon shots would always land in the divots he had made in the morning. He was such a naturally graceful and smooth swinger of the club that he inspired hundreds of golfers to imitate him and few players before or since have had such a wide-ranging impact on the game.

THE LOWEST OF THE LOW

The Open has been won eighteen times with aggregate seventy-two-hole scores that have beaten the 280 barrier:

1950, Troon
BOBBY LOCKE *(South Africa)*   69–72–70–68   279

1957, St Andrews
BOBBY LOCKE *(South Africa)*   69–72–68–70   279

1958, Royal Lytham
PETER THOMSON *(Australia)*   66–72–67–73   278*

1960, St Andrews
KEL NAGLE *(Australia)*   69–67–71–71   278

1962, Troon
ARNOLD PALMER *(USA)*   71–69–67–69   276

1963, Royal Lytham
BOB CHARLES *(New Zealand)*   68–72–66–71   277†

1964, St Andrews
TONY LEMA *(USA)*   73–68–68–70   279

1967, Hoylake
ROBERTO DE VICENZO *(Arg)*   70–71–67–70   278

1971, Birkdale
LEE TREVINO *(USA)*   69–70–69–70   278

1972, Muirfield
LEE TREVINO *(USA)*   71--70–66–71   278

1973, Troon
TOM WEISKOPF *(USA)*   68–67–71–70   276

1975, Carnoustie
TOM WATSON *(USA)*   71–67–69–72   279‡

1976, Birkdale
JOHNNY MILLER *(USA)*   72–68–73–66   279

1977, Turnberry
TOM WATSON *(USA)*   68–70–65–66   268

1980, Muirfield
TOM WATSON *(USA)*   68–70–64–69   271

1981, Sandwich
BILL ROGERS *(USA)*   72–66–67–71   276

1983, Birkdale
TOM WATSON *(USA)*   67–68–70–70   275

1984, St Andrews
SEVE BALLESTEROS *(Spain)*   69–68–70–69   276

*Thomson beat Dave Thomas (GB) in a play-off.
†Charles beat Phil Rodgers (USA) in a play-off.
‡Watson beat Jack Newton (AUS) in a play-off.

SO NEAR YET...

Twenty-three golfers have beaten the 280 barrier in the Open without the reward of the championship:

1958, Royal Lytham
DAVE THOMAS *(Great Britain)*   70−68−69−71   278
ERIC BROWN *(Great Britain)*   73−70−65−71   279
CHRISTY O'CONNOR *(Ireland)*   67−68−73−71   279

1960, St Andrews
ARNOLD PALMER *(USA)*   70−71−70−68   279

1963, Royal Lytham
PHIL RODGERS *(USA)*   67−68−73−69   277
JACK NICKLAUS *(USA)*   71−67−70−70   278

1971, Birkdale
LIANG HUAN LU *(Formosa)*   70−70−69−70   279

1972, Muirfield
JACK NICKLAUS *(USA)*   70−72−71−66   279

1973, Troon
JOHNNY MILLER *(USA)*   70−68−69−72   279
NEIL COLES *(Great Britain)*   71−72−70−66   279

1975, Carnoustie
JACK NEWTON *(Australia)*   69−71−65−74   279

1977, Turnberry
JACK NICKLAUS *(USA)*   68−70−65−66   269
HUBERT GREEN *(USA)*   72−66−74−67   279

1980, Muirfield
LEE TREVINO *(USA)*   68−67−71−69   275
BEN CRENSHAW *(USA)*   70−70−68−69   277

1983 Birkdale
HALE IRWIN *(USA)*   69−68−72−67   276
ANDY BEAN *(USA)*   70−69−70−67   276
GRAHAM MARSH *(Australia)*   69−70−74−64   277
LEE TREVINO *(USA)*   69−66−73−70   278
SEVE BALLESTEROS *(Spain)*   71−71−69−68   279
HAROLD HENNING *(South Africa)*   71−69−70−69   279

1984, St Andrews
TOM WATSON *(USA)*   71−68−66−73   278
BERNHARD LANGER *(W. Germany)*   71−68−68−71   278

Peter Thomson...collected £750 for his 1954 Open victory

THE SPIRALLING PRIZE MONEY

The total prize money in the Open has spiralled from £1000 in 1946 to £450,000 in the record-breaking year of 1984 when crowds of 187,753 at St Andrews made it the best-attended golf tournament of all time. Receipts topped one million pounds for the first time and the Open organizers, the Royal and Ancient, rewarded the players with a ten per cent increase in prize money. This list shows how the money has gone up and up and up.

1946: Total prize money £1000
Champion Sam Snead collected £150

1951: Total prize money £1700
Champion Max Faulkner collected £325

1954: Total prize money £3500
Champion Peter Thomson collected £750

1960: Total prize money £7000
Champion Kel Nagle collected £1250

1965: Total prize money £10,000
Champion Peter Thomson collected £1750

1969: Total prize money £30,000
Champion Tony Jacklin collected £4250

1975: Total prize money £76,000
Champion Tom Watson collected £7500

1977: Total prize money £102,000
Champion Tom Watson collected £10,000

1980: Total prize money £207,000
Champion Tom Watson collected £25,000

1984: Total prize money £450,000
Champion Seve Ballesteros collected £55,000

THE EXCLUSIVE SUB-66 CLUB

Twenty-two players have shot 65 or better during individual rounds in the Open.

63...MARK HAYES *(Great Britain)*
second round at Turnberry, 1977

63...ISAO AOKI *(Japan)*
third round at Muirfield, 1980

64...HORACIO CARBONETTI *(Argentina)*
second round at Muirfield, 1980

64...TOM WATSON *(USA)*
third round at Muirfield, 1980

64...HUBERT GREEN *(USA)*
third round at Muirfield, 1980

64...CRAIG STADLER *(USA)*
first round at Birkdale, 1983

64...GRAHAM MARSH *(Australia)*
fourth round at Birkdale, 1983

65...HENRY COTTON *(Great Britain)*
second round at Sandwich, 1934

65...LEOPOLDO RUIZ *(Argentina)*
second round at Royal Lytham, 1958

65...ERIC BROWN *(Great Britain)*
third round at Royal Lytham, 1958

65...PETER BUTLER *(Great Britain)*
second round at Muirfield, 1966

65...CHRISTY O'CONNOR Snr *(Ireland)*
second round at Royal Lytham, 1969

65...NEIL COLES *(Great Britain)*
first round at St Andrews, 1970

65...JACK NICKLAUS *(USA)*
fourth round at Troon, 1973

65...ANGEL GALLARDO *(Spain)*
second round at Turnberry, 1977

65...TOMMY HORTON *(Great Britain)*
third round at Turnberry, 1977

65...JACK NICKLAUS *(USA)*
third round at Turnberry, 1977

65...TOM WATSON *(USA)*
third round at Turnberry, 1977

65...TOM WATSON *(USA)*
fourth round at Turnberry, 1977

65...BILL LONGMUIR *(Great Britain)*
first round at Royal Lytham, 1979

65...SEVE BALLESTEROS *(Spain)*
second round at Royal Lytham, 1979

65...GORDON BRAND *(Great Britain)*
second round at Sandwich, 1981

Mark Hayes...scorched round Turnberry in 63 strokes

ON CLOUD NINE

Seventeen golfers have completed nine holes — going out or coming back — during Open championships. Scotland's Eric Brown achieved the feat twice in successive years. The finishing eighteen-hole score is in brackets.

28...DENIS DURNIAN *(Great Britain)*
First nine at Birkdale, 1983 (66)

29...TOM HALIBURTON *(Great Britain)*
First nine at Royal Lytham, 1963 (68)
PETER THOMSON *(Australia)*
First nine at Royal Lytham, 1963 (63)
TONY JACKLIN *(Great Britain)*
First nine at St Andrews, 1970 (67)
BILL LONGMUIR *(Great Britain)*
First nine at Royal Lytham (65)

30...ERIC BROWN *(Great Britain)*
First nine at St Andrews, 1957 (67)
ERIC BROWN *(Great Britain)*
Second nine at Royal Lytham (65)
LEOPOLDO RUIZ *(Argentina)*
First nine at Royal Lytham (65)
PHIL RODGERS *(USA)*
Second nine at Muirfield (70)
PETER ALLISS *(Great Britain)*
First nine at Royal Lytham (66)
JIMMY KINSELLA *(Ireland)*
First nine at Birkdale (68)
HARRY BANNERMAN *(Great Britain)*
First nine at Muirfield (67)
BERT YANCEY *(USA)*
First nine at Troon, 1973 (69)
CHRISTY O'CONNOR Jnr *(Ireland)*
First nine at Birkdale, 1976 (69)
ARNOLD PALMER *(USA)*
Second nine at Turnberry, 1977 (67)
JACK NICKLAUS *(USA)*
First nine at Royal Lytham, 1979 (69)
TOM WATSON *(USA)*
Second nine at Muirfield, 1980 (64)
LEE TREVINO *(USA)*
First nine at Birkdale, 1983 (66)

JUST FOR THE RECORD

The record lowest rounds for each championship course set during Open competition:

Prestwick:
69 by MACDONALD SMITH *(USA)*, 1925

St Andrews:
65 by NEIL COLES *(Great Britain)*, 1970

Muirfield:
63 by ISAO AOKI *(Japan)*, 1980

Hoylake:
67 by ROBERTO DE VICENZO *(Arg)* and GARY PLAYER *(South Africa)*, 1967

Sandwich:
65 by HENRY COTTON *(Great Britain)*, 1934; GORDON BRAND *(Great Britain)*, 1981

Royal Lytham:
65 by ERIC BROWN *(Great Britain)* and LEOPOLDO RUIZ *(Arg)*, 1958; CHRISTY O'CONNOR Jnr *(Ireland)*, 1969; BILL LONGMUIR *(Great Britain)* and SEVE BALLESTEROS *(Spain)*, 1979

Prince's:
68 by ARTHUR HAVERS *(Great Britain)*, 1932

Royal Birkdale:
66 by PETER OOSTERHUIS *(Great Britain)*, 1971; JOHNNY MILLER *(USA)* and MARK JAMES *(Great Britain)*, 1976

Carnoustie:
65 by JACK NEWTON *(Australia)*, 1975

Royal Troon:
65 by JACK NICKLAUS *(USA)*, 1973

Turnberry:
63 by MARK HAYES *(Great Britain)*, 1977

Deal:
71 by GEORGE DUNCAN *(Great Britain)* and LEN HOLLAND *(Great Britain)*, 1920

Musselburgh:
77 by WILLIE PARK Jnr *(Great Britain)* and ANDREW KIRKALDY *(Great Britain)*, 1889

Royal Portrush
68 by JIMMY ADAMS *(Great Britain)*, CHARLIE WARD *(Great Britain)* and NORMAN VON NIDA *(New Zealand)*, 1951

VERY CLOSE OPENS

Twelve Opens have finished tied, with eleven being decided by a play-off and another by a walk-over. All the ties have involved two competitors. There has yet to be a three-way tie.

DAVID STRATH tied on 176 with **BOB MARTIN** at St Andrews in 1876. An objection was lodged against Strath because in his final round he had played on to a green before the previous pairing had finished. No ruling was given and Strath withdrew, leaving Martin to walk over the course to clinch the championship.

BOB FERGUSON, bidding for his fourth consecutive title triumph, tied on 159 with **WILLIE FERNIE** at Musselburgh in 1883. They were level as they stood on the final tee in their thirty-six-hole play-off. Fernie drove the green and one-putted for victory by 158−159. He would have been the outright winner but for a ten on his card, the only time the winner of a major championship has recorded double figures for one hole.

WILLIE PARK Jnr beat **ANDREW KIRKALDY** by five strokes in a thirty-six-hole play-off (158−163) after they had tied on 155 at Musselburgh in 1889.

HARRY VARDON and **J.H. TAYLOR**, two legendary figures of golf, tied on 316 at Muirfield in 1896. Vardon won the play-off by four shots (157−161) to stop a championship hat-trick by Taylor and to win the first of his record six Open titles.

Frenchman **ARNAUD MASSY**, the first overseas winner of the championship in 1907, tied with **HARRY VARDON** on 303 at Sandwich in 1911. Massy conceded defeat at the thirty-fifth hole of the play-off with Vardon holding a lead of seven strokes.

ROGER WETHERED, bidding to become the third amateur winner of the Open, was penalized one shot for stepping on his ball at St Andrews in 1921. At the end of the seventy-two-hole tournament he was tied on 296 with Scots-born **JOCK HUTCH-ISON**, who won the play-off by nine strokes (150−159) to become he first American-based winner of the championship.

DENSMORE SHUTE beat **CRAIG WOOD** by five shots (149−154) in an all-American play-off for the championship at St Andrews in 1933 after they had tied on 292. Shute scored 73−73−73−73 to become the only champion to win with four carbon-copy rounds.

BOBBY LOCKE won the first of his four titles by beating Irishman **HARRY BRADSHAW** by twelve shots (135−147) at Sandwich in 1949 after they had tied on 283. This was the championship in which Bradshaw drove his ball into the neck of a broken beer bottle during the second round and played it as it lay, a shot that no doubt cost him the title (see Just Amazing section).

PETER THOMSON beat Britain's **DAVE THOMAS** 139−143 for his fourth victory in five years after they had tied on 278 at Royal Lytham in 1958.

BOB CHARLES became the first New Zealander and the first left-hander to win the Open when he beat **PHIL RODGERS** 140−148 in a play-off after they had tied on 277 at Royal Lytham in 1963. It was the last play-off decided over thirty-six holes.

DOUG SANDERS missed the chance to become outright champion when he three-putted the final green at St Andrews in 1970. This left him tied with **JACK NICKLAUS** on 283. The 'Golden Bear' drove through the eighteenth green with a prodigious tee shot in the play-off and got down in a birdie three to win by one shot (72−73).

JACK NEWTON, boosted by a third round 65, forced a play-off with **TOM WATSON** at Carnoustie in 1975 when they tied on 279. Watson won the eighteen-hole decider by one stroke (71−72) to win the first of his five Open titles.

THE GREAT INVADERS

Twenty-five overseas players have won the Open since Frenchman Arnaud Massy took the title across the Channel in 1907.

ARNAUD MASSY *(France)*	1907
JOCK HUTCHISON *(USA)*	1921*
WALTER HAGEN *(USA)*	1922—24—28—29
JIM BARNES *(USA)*	1925
BOBBY JONES *(USA)*	1926—27—30
TOMMY ARMOUR *(USA)*	1931*
GENE SARAZEN *(USA)*	1932
DENSMORE SHUTE *(USA)*	1933
SAM SNEAD *(USA)*	1946
BOBBY LOCKE *(South Africa)*	1949—50—52—57
BEN HOGAN *(USA)*	1953
PETER THOMSON *(Australia)*	1954—55—56—58—65
GARY PLAYER *(South Africa)*	1959—68—74
KEL NAGLE *(Australia)*	1960
ARNOLD PALMER *(USA)*	1961—62
BOB CHARLES *(New Zealand)*	1963
TONY LEMA *(USA)*	1964
JACK NICKLAUS *(USA)*	1966—70—78
ROBERTO DE VICENZO *(Arg)*	1967
LEE TREVINO *(USA)*	1971—72
TOM WEISKOPF *(USA)*	1973
TOM WATSON *(USA)*	1975—77—80—82—83
JOHNNY MILLER *(USA)*	1976
SEVE BALLESTEROS *(Spain)*	1979—84
BILL ROGERS *(USA)*	1981

*Born in Scotland

Bill Rogers...a winning invader at Sandwich in 1981

THE CROWDS AND THE CASH

Official attendances and gate monies for the Open have been kept since 1962.

Year	Course	Attendance	Receipts £
1962	Troon	37,098	15,207
1963	Royal Lytham	24,585	14,173
1964	St Andrews	35,954	14,704
1965	Royal Birkdale	32,927	21,214
1966	Muirfield	40,182	23,075
1967	Hoylake	29,880	20,180
1968	Carnoustie	51,819	31,907
1969	Royal Lytham	46,001	46,188
1970	St Andrews	81,593	62,744
1971	Royal Birkdale	70,076	90,052
1972	Muirfield	84,746	98,925
1973	Troon	78,810	115,000*
1974	Royal Lytham	92,796	158,729
1975	Carnoustie	85,258	176,012
1976	Royal Birkdale	92,021	243,793
1977	Turnberry	87,615	249,073
1978	St Andrews	125,271	421,474
1979	Royal Lytham	134,501	467,924
1980	Muirfield	131,610	538,288
1981	Sandwich	114,522	599,100
1982	Troon	133,299	665,000
1983	Royal Birkdale	142,894	794,000
1984	St Andrews	187,753	1,100,000*

Note: The 38,484 attendance on the second day of the 1984 Open at St Andrews is the highest single-day crowd figure at any championship.

*Approximate. VAT is not included in the final figures.

163

THAT WAS THE YEAR THAT WAS
Milestone Highlights in the History of the Open

1860: The first Open championship was staged at Prestwick over thirty-six holes on Wednesday, 17 October. Eight professionals were invited to take part by the Prestwick Golf Club with a championship belt as a prize for the winner. All the competitors were Scottish, with George Brown (Royal Blackheath Club) the one exile. Willie Park Snr was the winner, beating his constant rival 'Old' Tom Morris by two shots with a score of 174 for three rounds of the twelve-hole course. One of the also-rans recorded 21 at one hole, a score that has never been topped on any subsequent Open card. For the record the other five competitors were Robert Anderson, Alexander Smith, Willie Steel, Charles Hunter and Andrew Strath.

1862: 'Old' Tom Morris retained the championship belt he had won in 1861 and his winning victory margin of thirteen strokes is a record that still stands.

1863: Prize money was presented for the first time but not to the winner, Willie Park Snr. He received the championship belt, while the runner-up collected £5. The third man got £3 and the fourth £2. There were fourteen entrants.

1864: 'Old' Tom Morris won for a third time in the year that he resigned his custodianship of the Prestwick Links and returned to St Andrews as greenkeeper, a job he retained for forty years.

1865: Andrew Strath interrupted the Morris-Park domination of the championship with a record 162 score for the thirty-six holes. There were ten entrants and official scorecards were used for the first time.

1866: Willie Park Snr, the first champion, retained the title when he beat his brother, David, into second place. There were twelve entrants.

1868: 'Young' Tom Morris, just seventeen years old, succeeded his father as champion and his victory included the Open's first hole-in-one.

1870: 'Young' Tom Morris triumphed for the third successive year and so won the championship belt outright. His thirty-hole total of 149 was never beaten with a gutta-percha ball ('gutty').

164

1872: Following a year when there was no championship, 'Young' Tom Morris won for a fourth consecutive time which is a record that has never been equalled. He became the first winner of the new championship trophy, a silver claret jug. It was jointly presented by the Prestwick Club, the Royal and Ancient and the Honourable Company of Edinburgh Golfers who between them took over the organization of the championship. It was agreed that in future the Open would be staged in turn at the links at Prestwick, St Andrews and Musselburgh.

1873: The first Open at St Andrews after twelve championships had been staged at Prestwick. There was a record entry of twenty-six and Tom Kidd, a St Andrews caddie, was the winner.

1880: Bob Ferguson stopped a run of three successive victories by Jamie Anderson on the Musselburgh course where he had been a caddie, and he then went on to complete a hat-trick of Open wins.

1890: John Ball, who had first competed in the Open at the age of seventeen in 1878, won the Open to complete a double first — the first English winner and the first amateur champion. The son of an accomplished golfer from Hoylake, he won the British Amateur championship in the same year as his Open triumph which is a feat equalled only by Bobby Jones.

1892: Muirfield, replacing Musselbrough as the headquarters of the Honourable Company of Edinburgh Golfers, staged the Open for the first time. The competition was extended to seventy-two holes, with thirty-six holes being played on two successive days. Amateur Harold Hilton became the second amateur to collect the championship trophy.

1894: There was a record entry of ninety-four competitors at Sandwich for the first Open staged outside Scotland. J.H. Taylor scored the first of his five victories.

1898: Harry Vardon became the first Open champion to win the title with four rounds under 80. It was the second of his record six titles.

1899: First prize for the winner, Harry Vardon, was raised to £50 following the threat of strike action by many of the professionals.

1904: Jack White won the championship at Sandwich with a score of 296, the first seventy-two-hole total under 300. James Braid became the first to go under 70 for eighteen holes with a third-round 69, and in the final round J.H. Taylor lowered the record to 68. Braid and Taylor were joint second on 297.

1906: The Great Triumvirate of Braid, Taylor and Vardon finished first, second and third. It was Braid's second successive win and the third of his five triumphs.

1907: Frenchman Arnaud Massy became the first overseas winner, beating a record field of 192 rivals at Hoylake. There was such a strong gale blowing during the competition that even the biggest hitters were having to take a wood to reach the green from the tee on the 158-yard fourth. Qualifying rounds were introduced for the first time.

1908: James Braid lowered the Open aggregate record to 291, beating his nearest challenger by eight shots.

1910: The Golden Jubilee of the championship. James Braid celebrated with his fifth victory and the prize money was increased to £125.

1912: Ted Ray, like Harry Vardon born on the island of Jersey, won the championship and eight years later added the U.S. Open to his collection. Vardon and Tony Jacklin are the only other British golfers to have achieved this double.

1914: Harry Vardon completed his record sixth victory. Two qualifying rounds were introduced. Because of the First World War it was the last championship for six years and when the Open was resumed in 1920 it was under the auspices of the Royal and Ancient Golf Club.

1920: George Duncan won the trophy and the record first prize of £100 with an astonishing comeback. He trailed Abe Mitchell by thirteen strokes after thirty-six holes but finished with a 71 and a 72 to take the title.

1921: For the first time the Open trophy was taken to the United States — by Scots-born Jock Hutchison who beat English amateur Roger Wethered in a play-off. A young American amateur called Bobby Jones tore up his card at the eleventh in the third round, bowing to the superiority of the St Andrews course.

1922: Walter Hagen won the first of his four championships and became the first of a long line of American-born golfers to dominate the Open. There was a record entry of 277 competitors when Hagen next won in 1924.

1925: The last Open at Prestwick where it had all started sixty-five years earlier. American Jim Barnes won following a last round collapse by Macdonald Smith who had needed a 78 to clinch victory but stumbled to a nightmare 82. Smith, born at Carnoustie but based in America, was rated one of the greatest golfers never to have won an Open.

1926: Bobby Jones won the first of his three Open championships. He was two down with five to play in the final round against his countryman and playing partner Al Watrous but cut the deficit with one miraculous shot at the seventeenth which is commemorated by a plaque on the Royal Lytham course at the point where he struck his 170-yard mashie-iron shot from sand to the green (see Just Amazing section). Jones finally won by two shots, with Walter Hagen back in third place.

1927: Bobby Jones retained his championship with a record aggregate total of 285 in a tournament now spread over three days. He had mastered the St Andrews course that brought him to his knees in 1921.

1928: The Prince of Wales presented the trophy to winner Walter Hagen, who won again the following year with a performance that included a 'faultless' round of 67.

1930: A third championship for Bobby Jones on his way to the Grand Slam in what was to be his last year in competitive golf. He had a seven at the 527-yard ninth without touching a bunker but recovered to win by two shots from Leo Diegel.

1931: The first Open staged at Carnoustie and won by Edinburgh-born, American-based Tommy Armour. Argentinian Jose Jurado, followed around the course by the Prince of Wales who had met him during a trip to South America, needed a 75 to clinch victory in the final round but took a 77 and finished a stroke behind Armour.

1932: Prince's at Sandwich was host for the Open for the one and only time. Gene Sarazen scored 70−69−70−74 for a record aggregate of 283 and a five-shot victory over perennial runner-up Macdonald Smith.

1933: Densmore Shute beat his countryman Craig Wood in a play-off in an Open that was dominated by Americans. They filled five of the first six places to wipe out the memory of a Ryder Cup defeat by Britain shortly before the championship at St Andrews. Leo Diegel, needing to sink a short putt to force a triple tie on the last green, missed the ball completely. Shute scored 73−73−73−73 for the four rounds, the only time a champion has won with identical scores for each round.

1934: Henry Cotton gave British golf a much-needed boost with a magnificent victory at Sandwich. He started with a 67, then carded a best-ever round of 65 and looked ready to rewrite the record books. But he faltered on the final round, scoring 79 that was good enough to give him victory by five shots and an equal all-time best aggregrate score of 283. There was a record entry of 312.

1935: This was the year of the Alfred the Greats – Alf Perry beating Alf Padgham by four shots for a surprise victory in a record-equalling 283.

1936: Victory this time for Alf Padgham following a second and third place in the previous two Opens. His clubs were locked in the club shop on the final day and there was no key. He smashed a window and retrieved them just in time to get to the tee for the final round (see What A Carry On).

1937: The entire U.S. Ryder Cup team entered but were unable to match the brilliance of Henry Cotton who clinched his second championship with a final round of 71 after trailing behind brothers Reg and Charles Whitcombe who finished second and fourth respectively.

1938: Reg Whitcombe defied gale-force winds and storms on the final day to win by two strokes from Jimmy Adams of Liverpool. An indication of the strength of the wind is that Alf Padgham drove the green at the 380-yard eleventh and one-putted for an eagle two.

1939: Dick Burton recovered from a third round 77 to win by two strokes from American Johnny Bulla. His round-by-round score was 70–72–77–71 and he wrapped up the title with a birdie three at the eighteenth following a magnificent 340-yard drive.

1946: Slammin' Sam Snead totalled 290 to win the first Open after the Second World War, with Johnny Bulla and Bobby Locke tied on second place four strokes behind.

1947: Fred Daly became the first Irishman to win the Open despite a third round 78 that threatened to end his hopes. American amateur Frank 'Muscles' Stranahan very nearly forced a play-off with a 150-yard shot to the final green that finished just inches from the hole. On the same green Daly had sunk a putt from twelve yards that gave him a one-stroke victory over Stranahan and Reg Horne.

1948: Watched by George V1, Henry Cotton produced golf fit to put before a king to win his third championship. 'King Henry' totalled 284 to beat defending champion Fred Daly by four strokes.

1949: Bobby Locke recorded the first of his four victories, beating Harry Bradshaw in a play-off after they had tied on 283. Bradshaw might have won outright but for having to play his ball from an 'impossible' lie in the neck of a broken beer bottle.

1950: Bobby Locke retained the championship and lowered the record aggregate to 279 with an impressive 69−72−70−68 sequence. Roberto de Vicenzo (281), Fred Daly (282) and Dai Rees (282) were also inside the old record.

1951: Max Faulkner interrupted the Locke monopoly on the Portrush course in Ireland, the only time the Open has not been held in either Scotland or England. The colourful Faulkner collected £325 as his share of the new record total of £1700. He was to prove Britain's last victor for eighteen years.

1952: Bobby Locke won his third Open in four years after being instructed to speed up his game following complaints about his slow play. Peter Thomson, a twenty-two-year-old Australian, was second just a stroke behind on 288.

1953: Ben Hogan added the Open to his U.S. and Masters successes, becoming the first player to complete this treble in the same year. He shot ever-improving scores of 73−71−70−68 to win with four strokes to spare. It was the one and only time he played the British Open.

1954: Peter Thomson became the first Australian to win the Open in the first championship staged at Birkdale. He totalled 283, one ahead of Bobby Locke, Syd Scott and Dai Rees. It was the second successive year that Rees had finished joint runner-up.

1955: Peter Thomson retained the title and picked up a record cheque of £1000. BBC TV cameras provided live coverage for the first time. Thomson's 281 beat the previous St Andrews Open record set by Bobby Jones by four shots.

1956: Peter Thomson completed the first hat-trick of modern times. It was a bleak Open for British golfers, with John Panton the highest finisher in fifth place.

1957: The Open venue was switched to St Andrews from Muirfield because of petrol rationing following the Suez crisis. Bobby Locke beat Peter Thomson by three shots for his fourth championship, escaping a penalty when he placed his ball on the wrong spot for his final putt (see Just Amazing section). It was the first year in which the leaders went out last for the final two rounds, no doubt to provide more compelling viewing as television coverage became an accepted part of the Open.

1958: Peter Thomson and Britain's Dave Thomas tied on a new record aggregate score of 278. Thomson won the play-off for his fourth championship in five years, a success sequence equalled only by 'Young' Tom Morris in the last century.

1959: Gary Player won for the first time despite a nervous first round of 75 and a traumatic six on the final hole that he was convinced had cost him the championship. His winning sequence was 75−71−70−68. Only Ben Hogan (1953), Jack White (1904) and James Braid (1906) had previously won the championship with an improved score in each of the four rounds. Belgian Flory van Donck, equal second with Fred Bullock, had proved the most consistent continental challenger since Frenchman Arnaud Massy more than fifty years earlier. For the first time, total prize money reached £5000.

1960: A violent storm washed out play on the last afternoon of the centenary championship at St Andrews and the final round was put back to the Saturday. Australian Kel Nagle was a surprise winner, with a record-equalling 278. He held off a last-round charge from an American making his first challenge for the championship. His name: Arnold Palmer, who finished second, one shot behind Nagle. There were a record 410 entrants.

1961: Arnold Palmer's genius for the game rose above the gales that wrecked the performances of lesser players and he took his first Open with a score of 284, one stroke ahead of that gallant Welsh battler Dai Rees. One of Palmer's more spectacular shots is commemorated with a plaque just off the sixth fairway at Royal Birkdale (see Just Amazing section). For the second successive year a storm forced the abandonment of the Friday programme and the final round was switched to the Saturday.

1962: Arnold Palmer held on to the championship in great style, winning by six strokes in a record 276 (71−69−67−69). A chubby young American called Jack Nicklaus made his Open debut and he finished equal thirty-fourth with Eric Brown after a painful first round of 80 that included a ten at the eleventh.

1963: Bob Charles created history when he became the first left hander and the first New Zealander to win the Open following a play-off with Phil Rodgers. Charles and Rodgers tied on 277, with Jack Nicklaus third one stroke behind.

1964: Tony Lema, making his Open debut, arrived just the day before the championship and played St Andrews 'blind', relying on his caddie to point him in the right direction. Lema won by five strokes from Jack Nicklaus who completed the last two rounds in a record 134 (66−68).

1965: Peter Thomson completed his fifth and most satisfying Open triumph, beating a top-quality field that included American giants Arnold Palmer and Jack Nicklaus. He had trailed defending champion Tony Lema by six strokes at the end of the first round (68 to 74) but then produced a procession of superb iron shots for a 68–72–71 sequence that gave him victory by two strokes from Brian Huggett and Christy O'Connor Snr.

1966: Jack Nicklaus mastered a wickedly difficult Muirfield course that was thigh-deep in rough and won his first Open by one stroke (282) from Doug Sanders and – runner-up for a second time – Dave Thomas. It completed the first of the 'Golden Bear's' three Grand Slams.

1967: A triumph at last for 'Try-Try-and-Try-Again' Roberto de Vicenzo, who at forty-four was the oldest winner of the championship. In twenty years of bidding for the title the popular Argentinian had finished second in 1950, third four times, fourth and sixth. He produced a third-round 67 that made him the first golfer in an Open to beat 70 at Hoylake. De Vicenzo completed the seventy-two holes in 278, two strokes ahead of Jack Nicklaus.

1968: Carnoustie provided one of the most challenging of all Opens with a longest-ever championship course of 7252 yards. Gary Player was one of the few players to keep a six off his card in a high-scoring tournament in which only Jack Nicklaus (69) and Billy Casper (68) broke 70. Player finally won his second championship with an aggregate of 289, the highest winning score for twenty-one years. Nicklaus and Bob Charles tied for second place on 291.

1969: Tony Jacklin became Britain's first winner for eighteen years, the longest barren stretch without a British championship victory. Jacklin collected the record first prize of £4250 with a 62–70–70–72 sequence for a finishing score of 280. Former Open champions Bob Charles (second on 282), Roberto de Vicenzo, Peter Thomson, Jack Nicklaus, Kel Nagle, Gary Player and Max Faulkner – the last British victor – trailed in Jacklin's wake.

1970: This is always remembered as the Open that Doug Sanders lost rather than the one that Jack Nicklaus won. Sanders missed a simple putt on the final green to leave himself tied with Nicklaus who won a dramatic eighteen-hole play-off by one stroke, clinching his second championship with a spectacular birdie three at the final hole.

1971: Lee Trevino won the 100th Open to complete an amazing hat-trick. In the previous four weeks he had captured the U.S. and Canadian Open titles. He finished one stroke ahead of polite

Roberto de Vicenzo...for whom perseverance paid off

Formosan Lu Liang Huan, whose second place was the highest position ever by an Asian golfer.

1972: Lee Trevino retained the title thanks to some miraculous shots in the last round that broke the challenge of Tony Jacklin. Trevino holed from a bunker and sank two chip shots as he finished with five consecutive birdies for a score of 278 and victory by one stroke from Jack Nicklaus. Jacklin, who had been looking a potential winner, slipped back to third place as he watched his playing partner Trevino working his magic. The total prize money was increased to £50,000.

1973: Tom Weiskopf played eight practice rounds over the Troon course in a thorough preparation for his Open challenge and he proved that practice can make perfect when he equalled the championship record score of 276 to take the title by three shots from Neil Coles and Johnny Miller.

1974: The 'big' ball (1.68 inches in diameter compared to 1.62 inches) was made compulsory and Gary Player immediately made a big impact with opening rounds of 69 and 68. Player faltered with a third-round 75 but then produced a stylish 70 to clinch his third championship with four strokes to spare over runner-up Peter Oosterhuis (286).

1975: Tom Watson won the first of his five Open championships on a Carnoustie course that presented none of the problems that wrecked so many cards in 1968. There were a spate of sub-70 rounds and several players, including Bobby Cole, Jack Nicklaus, Johnny Miller, Graham Marsh, Peter Oosterhuis, Neil Coles and Jack Newton, took turns in looking likely champions. Watson arrived at the last minute for his first Open challenge and relied on caddie Alfie Fyles to steer him round the course. He and Newton were tied on 279 at the end of a dramatic final round and Watson won the play-off 71−72.

1976: Johnny Miller finished a comfortable winner by six strokes but not before a young nineteen-year-old Spaniard called Seve-riano Ballesteros had threatened to run away with the title with opening rounds of 69 and 69. Seve finally finished joint second with Jack Nicklaus but had given notice of great things to come.

1977: Many consider the first Open staged at Turnberry the greatest championship in living memory. It featured a memorable head-to-head duel between Jack Nicklaus and Tom Watson that was stretched over two full days and was not settled until the final hole. Watson finally pipped Nicklaus by one shot in a new aggregate record of 268. They matched each other shot for shot, birdie for birdie and had identical scores over the first three rounds — 68—70—65. Watson then unleashed another 65 to a 66 by Nicklaus. It was the lowest ever final round by a champion in an Open dripping with records. Americans filled eleven of the first twelve positions, Mark Hayes set a new eighteen-hole low of 63, there were eleven sub-67 rounds, total prize money was £100,000 and there was a Scottish record crowd of 92,200.

1978: Jack Nicklaus captured his third championship and his second at St Andrews thanks to stunning finishing rounds of 69 and 69 that gave him a winning aggregate of 281. New Zealander Simon Owen gave him a close battle over the final eighteen holes and finally finished tied for second place on 283 with American aces Raymond Floyd, Ben Crenshaw and Tom Kite.

1979: Severiano Ballesteros became the first Spaniard to win the Open and the first continental since Frenchman Arnaud Massy in 1907. Ballesteros equalled the course record with a 65 in the second round and in the final two rounds made a staggering series of brilliant recovery shots after continually missing the fairway with his unpredictable drives. Jack Nicklaus was runner-up for a record seventh time and Ben Crenshaw, as in 1978, was equal second, three shots behind Ballesteros who finished on 283. Mark James was Britain's best-placed player in fourth place and Bill Longmuir lit up the first round with a course record equalling 65 that included an outward half in 29.

1980: Tom Watson's third Open championship victory included a third round of 64, a record for a winner of the title. There has rarely been a third round quite like it for record scoring in a major championship. Isao Aoki equalled the best-ever Open eighteen-hole score with a 63 and Hubert Green totalled 64 on a day when seventeen players broke the '70' barrier. Watson's winning sequence was 68—70—64—69 for an aggregate 271 and a four-shot advantage over runner-up Lee Trevino. For the first time there was a scheduled Sunday finish.

1981: Bill Rogers won his first major championship with an aggregate score of 276, four ahead of runner-up Bernhard Langer. Strong winds at Sandwich wrecked many scorecards but Rogers played controlled golf to become the only player to beat par for the four rounds.

1982: Tom Watson was handed his fourth Open after both Nick Price and Bobby Clampett had tossed away excellent victory chances. Watson's aggregate of 284 gave him the title by one stroke from joint runner-up Price and Peter Oosterhuis. Clampett had started with a 67 and a 68 and held a five-stroke lead at the halfway stage over Price and was seven strokes ahead of Watson. But he

Isao Aoki...equalled the Open record with a 63

then struggled through rounds of 78 and 77. There were a record 1121 entrants and Watson's first prize was £32,000.

1983: Tom Watson won his fifth Open in nine attempts for a record that rivals the best in the history of the championship. It was a thrilling climax at Birkdale with just five shots covering the first eleven players. Watson's 67−68−70−70 sequence gave him a winning aggregate of 275, one ahead of Hale Irwin and Andy Bean.

1984: Severiano Ballesteros collected a record first prize of £55,000 as reward for winning his second Open with an aggregate of 276, two ahead of defending champion Tom Watson and Bernhard Langer. There were record crowds at St Andrews of 187,753 and receipts from ticket sales topped one million pounds for the first time.

JIMMY GREAVES
How I Would Like To Play the Game

I would consider myself the perfect golfer if I could have...

The **DRIVE** of **GREG NORMAN**
The **SWING** of **SAM SNEAD**
The **LONG IRONS** game of **JACK NICKLAUS**
The **SHORT IRONS** game of **SEVE BALLESTEROS**
The **BUNKER SHOTS** of **GARY PLAYER**
The **PUTTING** of **TOM WATSON**
The **TEMPERAMENT** of **BEN HOGAN**

'If I had a combination of all these skills I reckon I would be about the greatest golfer that ever lived. The nearest to the perfect golfer in my lifetime has been Jack Nicklaus, although old-timers tell me that Bobby Jones was in a class of his own. Arnold Palmer is the player I always most enjoyed watching. He had an enthusiasm for the game that radiated itself to the spectators.'

JIMMY GREAVES is rated by many good judges to have been the greatest goalscorer of modern times. He scored a record 357 First Division goals during his League career with Chelsea, Tottenham and West Ham. In 57 England international matches he scored 44 goals, a total beaten only by Bobby Charlton (49 goals in 106 games). Jimmy, a keen golfer when time allows, has built a new career for himself as a television personality whose outspoken views on football are always entertaining as well as enlightening.

SECTION SEVEN
THE CHAMPIONS

Winners of the four major championships, The Open, U.S. Open, U.S. PGA and U.S. Masters:

THE OPEN CHAMPIONSHIP

Year	Champion	Score	Venue
1860	Willie Park (GB)	174	Prestwick
1861	Tom Morris Snr (GB)	163	Prestwick
1862	Tom Morris Snr (GB)	163	Prestwick
1863	Willie Park (GB)	168	Prestwick
1864	Tom Morris Snr (GB)	167	Prestwick
1865	Andrew Strath (GB)	162	Prestwick
1866	Willie Park (GB)	169	Prestwick
1867	Tom Morris Snr (GB)	170	Prestwick
1868	Tom Morris Jnr (GB)	157	Prestwick
1869	Tom Morris Jnr (GB)	154	Prestwick
1870	Tom Morris Jnr (GB)	149	Prestwick

Tom Morris Jnr won the belt outright. There was no championship in 1871 and it was resumed in 1872 with the introduction of the Cup

Year	Champion	Score	Venue
1872	Tom Morris Jnr (GB)	166	Prestwick
1873	Tom Kidd (GB)	179	St Andrews
1874	Mungo Park (GB)	159	Musselburgh
1875	Willie Park (GB)	166	Prestwick
1876	Bob Martin (GB)	176	St Andrews
1877	Jamie Anderson (GB)	160	Musselburgh
1878	Jamie Anderson (GB)	157	Prestwick
1879	Jamie Anderson (GB)	169	St Andrews
1880	Bob Ferguson (GB)	162	Musselburgh
1881	Bob Ferguson (GB)	170	Prestwick
1882	Bob Ferguson (GB)	171	St Andrews
1883	Willie Fernie (GB)	159	Musselburgh
1884	Jack Simpson (GB)	160	Prestwick
1885	Bob Martin (GB)	171	St Andrews
1886	David Brown (GB)	157	Musselburgh
1887	Willie Park Jnr (GB)	161	Prestwick
1888	Jack Burns (GB)	171	St Andrews
1889	Willie Park Jnr (GB)	155	Musselburgh
1890	John Ball (GB), amateur	164	Prestwick
1891	Hugh Kirkaldy (GB)	166	St Andrews

The competition was extended from 36 holes to 72 holes in 1892

Year	Champion	Score	Venue
1892	Harold Hilton (GB), amateur	305	Muirfield
1893	Willie Auchterlonie (GB)	322	Prestwick
1894	J.H. Taylor (G.B.)	326	Sandwich
1895	J.H. Taylor (GB)	322	St Andrews
1896	Harry Vardon (GB)	316	Muirfield
1897	Harold Hilton (GB), amateur	314	Hoylake
1898	Harry Vardon (GB)	307	Prestwick
1899	Harry Vardon (GB)	310	Sandwich
1900	J.H. Taylor (GB)	309	St Andrews
1901	James Braid (GB)	309	Muirfield
1902	Alex Herd (GB)	307	Hoylake
1903	Harry Vardon (GB)	300	Prestwick
1904	Jack White (GB)	296	Sandwich
1905	James Braid (GB)	318	St Andrews
1906	James Braid (GB)	300	Muirfield
1907	Arnaud Massy (France)	312	Hoylake
1908	James Braid (GB)	291	Prestwick
1909	J.H. Taylor (GB)	295	Deal
1910	James Braid (GB)	299	St Andrews
1911	Harry Vardon (GB)	303	Sandwich
1912	Ted Ray (GB)	295	Muirfield
1913	J.H. Taylor (GB)	304	Hoylake
1914	Harry Vardon (GB)	306	Prestwick
1915−19	*No championship due to the war*		
1920	George Duncan (GB)	303	Deal
1921	Jock Hutchison (USA)	296	St Andrews
1922	Walter Hagen (USA)	300	Sandwich
1923	A.G. Havers (GB)	295	Troon
1924	Walter Hagen (USA)	301	Hoylake
1925	Jim Barnes (USA)	300	Prestwick
1926	Bobby Jones (USA), amateur	291	Royal Lytham
1927	Bobby Jones (USA), amateur	285	St Andrews
1928	Walter Hagen (USA)	292	Sandwich
1929	Walter Hagen (USA)	292	Muirfield
1930	Bobby Jones (USA), amateur	291	Hoylake
1931	Tommy Armour (USA)	296	Carnoustie
1932	Gene Sarazen (USA)	283	Prince's, Sandwich
1933	Densmore Shute (USA)	292	St Andrews
1934	Henry Cotton (GB)	283	Sandwich
1935	Alf Perry (GB)	282	Muirfield
1936	Alf Padgham (GB)	287	Hoylake
1937	Henry Cotton (GB)	290	Carnoustie
1938	Reg Whitcombe (GB)	295	Sandwich
1939	Dick Burton (GB)	290	St Andrews
1940−45	*No championship due to the war*		

Year	Champion	Score	Venue
1946	Sam Snead (USA)	290	St Andrews
1947	Fred Daly (GB)	293	Hoylake
1948	Henry Cotton (GB)	284	Muirfield
1949	Bobby Locke (South Africa)	283	Sandwich
1950	Bobby Locke (South Africa)	279	Troon
1951	Max Faulkner (GB)	285	Portrush
1952	Bobby Locke (South Africa)	287	Royal Lytham
1953	Ben Hogan (USA)	282	Carnoustie
1954	Peter Thomson (Australia)	283	Royal Birkdale
1955	Peter Thomson (Australia)	281	St Andrews
1956	Peter Thomson (Australia)	286	Hoylake
1957	Bobby Locke (South Africa)	279	St Andrews
1958	Peter Thomson (Australia)	278	Royal Lytham
1959	Gary Player (South Africa)	284	Muirfield
1960	Kel Nagle (Australia)	278	St Andrews
1961	Arnold Palmer (USA)	284	Royal Birkdale
1962	Arnold Palmer (USA)	276	Troon
1963	Bob Charles (New Zealand)	277	Royal Lytham
1964	Tony Lema (USA)	279	St Andrews
1965	Peter Thomson (Australia)	285	Royal Birkdale
1966	Jack Nicklaus (USA)	282	Muirfield
1967	Roberto de Vicenzo (Arg.)	278	Hoylake
1968	Gary Player (South Africa)	289	Carnoustie
1969	Tony Jacklin (GB)	280	Royal Lytham
1970	Jack Nicklaus (USA)	283	St Andrews
1971	Lee Trevino (USA)	278	Royal Birkdale
1972	Lee Trevino (USA)	278	Muirfield
1973	Tom Weiskopf (USA)	276	Troon
1974	Gary Player (South Africa)	282	Royal Lytham
1975	Tom Watson (USA)	279	Carnoustie
1976	Johnny Miller (USA)	279	Royal Birkdale
1977	Tom Watson (USA)	268	Turnberry
1978	Jack Nicklaus (USA)	281	St Andrews
1979	Severiano Ballesteros (Spain)	283	Royal Lytham
1980	Tom Watson (USA)	271	Muirfield
1981	Bill Rogers (USA)	276	Sandwich
1982	Tom Watson (USA)	284	Troon
1983	Tom Watson (USA)	275	Royal Birkdale
1984	Severiano Ballesteros (Spain)	276	St Andrews

UNITED STATES OPEN CHAMPIONSHIP

Year	Champion		Venue
1894	Willie Dunn (USA), won by 2 holes		St Andrews, N.Y.

From 1895 the championship was decided by strokeplay. The winner was American-born, unless otherwise stated

Year	Champion	Score	Venue
1895	Horace Rawlins (GB)	173	Newport
1896	James Foulis (GB)	152	Southampton
1897	Joe Lloyd (GB)	162	Wheaton, Ill.

From 1898, the championship was extended from 36 holes to 72 holes

1898	Fred Herd (GB)	328	Shinnecock Hills
1899	Willie Smith (GB)	315	Baltimore
1900	Harry Vardon (GB)	315	Wheaton, Ill.
1901	Willie Anderson (GB)	315	Myopia, Mass.
1902	Laurie Auchterlonie (GB)	305	Garden City
1903	Willie Anderson (GB)	307	Baltusrol
1904	Willie Anderson (GB)	304	Glenview
1905	Willie Anderson (GB)	335	Myopia, Mass.
1906	Alex Smith (GB)	291	Onwentsia
1907	Alex Ross (GB)	302	Chestnut Hill, Pa.
1908	Freddie McLeod (GB)	322	Myopia, Mass.
1909	George Sargent (GB)	290	Englewood, N.J.
1910	Alex Smith (GB)	289	Philadelphia
1911	John McDermott	307	Wheaton, Ill.
1912	John McDermott	294	Buffalo, N.Y.
1913	Francis Ouimet, amateur	304	Brookline, Mass.
1914	Walter Hagen	297	Midlothian
1915	Jerry Travers, amateur	290	Baltusrol
1916	Charles Evans, amateur	286	Minneapolis
1917–18	*No championship due to the war*		
1919	Walter Hagen	303	Braeburn
1920	Ted Ray (GB)	295	Inverness
1921	Jim Barnes	289	Washington
1922	Gene Sarazen	288	Glencoe
1923	Bobby Jones, amateur	295	Inwood, L.I.
1924	Cyril Walker (GB)	297	Oakwood Hills

Year	Champion	Score	Venue
1925	Willie MacFarlane (GB)	291	Worcester
1926	Bobby Jones, amateur	293	Scioto, Ohio
1927	Tommy Armour (GB/USA)	301	Oakmont
1928	Johnny Farrell	294	Olympia Fields
1929	Bobby Jones, amateur	294	Winged Foot, N.Y.
1930	Bobby Jones, amateur	287	Interlachen
1931	Billie Burke	292	Inverness
1932	Gene Sarazen	286	Fresh Meadow
1933	Johnny Goodman, amateur	287	North Shore
1934	Olin Dutra	293	Merion
1935	Sam Parks Jnr	299	Oakmont
1936	Tony Manero	282	Baltusrol
1937	Ralph Guldahl	281	Oakland Hills
1938	Ralph Guldahl	284	Cherry Hills
1939	Byron Nelson	284	Philadelphia
1940	Lawson Little	287	Canterbury, Ohio
1941	Craig Wood	284	Fort Worth, Texas
1942–45	*Championship not played due to the war*		
1946	Lloyd Mangrum	284	Canterbury, Ohio
1947	Lew Worsham	282	St Louis
1948	Ben Hogan	276	Los Angeles
1949	Cary Middlecoff	286	Medinah
1950	Ben Hogan	287	Merion, Pa.
1951	Ben Hogan	287	Oakland Hills
1952	Julius Boros	281	Dallas, Texas
1953	Ben Hogan	283	Oakmont, Pa.
1954	Ed Furgol	284	Baltusrol
1955	Jack Fleck	287	San Francisco
1956	Cary Middelcoff	281	Rochester
1957	Dick Mayer	282	Inverness
1958	Tommy Bolt	283	Tulsa, Okl.
1959	Billy Casper	282	Winged Foot, N.Y.
1960	Arnold Palmer	280	Cherry Hills
1961	Gene Littler	281	Oakland Hills
1962	Jack Nicklaus	283	Oakmont, Pa.
1963	Julius Boros	293	Brookline, Mass.
1964	Ken Venturi	278	Washington
1965	Gary Player (South Africa)	282	St Louis
1966	Billy Casper	278	San Francisco
1967	Jack Nicklaus	275	Baltusrol
1968	Lee Trevino	275	Rochester
1969	Orville Moody	281	Houston, Texas
1970	Tony Jacklin (GB)	281	Chaska, Minn.
1971	Lee Trevino	280	Merion, Pa.
1972	Jack Nicklaus	290	Pebble Beach
1973	Johnny Miller	279	Oakmont, Pa.
1974	Hale Irwin	287	Winged Foot, N.Y.

184

Year	Champion	Score	Venue
1975	Lou Graham	287	Medinah, Ill.
1976	Jerry Pate	277	Atlanta
1977	Hubert Green	278	Southern Hills
1978	Andy North	285	Cherry Hills
1979	Hale Irwin	284	Inverness
1980	Jack Nicklaus	272	Baltusrol
1981	David Graham (Australia)	281	Merion, Pa.
1982	Tom Watson	282	Pebble Beach
1983	Larry Nelson	280	Oakmont, Pa.
1984	Fuzzy Zoeller	276	Winged Foot, N.Y.

UNITED STATES PGA CHAMPIONSHIP

Match play up until 1957, then switched to strokeplay

Year	Champion	Venue
1916	Jim Barnes, 1 hole	Siwanoy, N.Y.
1917–18	*No championship due to the war*	
1919	Jim. Barnes, 6 and 5	Engineers' Club, N.Y.
1920	Jock Hutchison, 1 hole	Flossmoor, Ill.
1921	Walter Hagen, 3 and 2	Inwood, N.Y.
1922	Gene Sarazen, 4 and 3	Oakmont, Pa.
1923	Gene Sarazen, 38th hole	Pelham, N.Y.
1924	Walter Hagen, 2 holes	French Lick, Ind.
1925	Walter Hagen, 6 and 4	Olympic Fields, Ill.
1926	Walter Hagen, 5 and 3	Salisbury, N.Y.
1927	Walter Hagen, 1 hole	Dallas, Texas
1928	Leo Diegel, 6 and 5	Baltimore
1929	Leo Diegel, 6 and 4	Hillcrest, Calif.
1930	Tommy Armour, 1 hole	Fresh Meadow, N.Y.
1931	Tom Creavy, 2 and 1	Wannamoisett, R.I.
1932	Olin Dutra, 4 and 3	St Paul, Minn.
1933	Gene Sarazen, 5 and 4	Milwaukee
1934	Paul Runyan, 38th hole	Buffalo, N.Y.
1935	John Revolta, 5 and 4	Oklahoma
1936	Denny Shute, 3 and 2	Pinehurst, N.C.
1937	Denny Shute, 37th hole	Pittsburgh, Pa.
1938	Paul Runyan, 8 and 7	Shawnee, Pa.
1939	Henry Picard, 37th hole	Pomonok, N.Y.
1940	Byron Nelson, 1 hole	Hershey, Pa.
1941	Vic Ghezzi, 38th hole	Cherry Hills, Col.
1942	Sam Snead, 2 and 1	Seaview, N.J.
1943	*No championship due to war*	
1944	Bob Hamilton, 1 hole	Spokane, Wash.
1945	Byron Nelson, 4 and 3	Dayton, Ohio
1946	Ben Hogan, 6 and 4	Portland, Oregon
1947	Jim Ferrier, 2 and 1	Detroit, Mich.
1948	Ben Hogan, 7 and 6	Norwood Hills, Mo.
1949	Sam Snead, 3 and 2	Richmond, VA.
1950	Chandler Harper, 4 and 3	Scioto, Ohio
1951	Sam Snead, 7 and 6	Oakmont, Pa.
1952	Jim Turnesa, 1 hole	Louisville, Ky.
1953	Walter Burkemo, 2 and 1	Birmingham, Mich.
1954	Chick Herbert, 4 and 3	St. Paul, Minn.
195	Doug Ford, 4 and 3	Detroit, Mich.
1956	Jack Burke, 3 and 2	Boston, Mass.
1957	Lionel Hebert, 3 and 1	Miami Valley, Ohio

Year	Champion	Score	Venue
1958	Dow Finsterwald	276	Havertown, Penn.
1959	Bob Rosburg	277	Minneapolis, Minn.
1960	Jay Hebert	281	Akron, Ohio
1961	Jerry Barber	277	Olympia Fields
1962	Gary Player (South Africa)	278	Aronimink, Pa.
1963	Jack Nicklaus	279	Dallas, Texas
1964	Bob Nichols	271	Columbus, Ohio
1965	Dave Marr	280	Ligonier, Penn.
1966	Al Geiberger	280	Akron, Ohio
1967	Don January	281	Denver, Col.
1968	Julius Boros	281	San Antonio, Texas
1969	Ray Floyd	276	Dayton, Ohio
1970	Dave Stockton	279	Tulsa, Okla.
1971	Jack Nicklaus	281	Palm Beach, Cal.
1972	Gary Player (South Africa)	281	Birmingham, Mich.
1973	Jack Nicklaus	277	Canterbury, Ohio
1974	Lee Trevino	276	Tanglewood, N.C.
1975	Jack Nicklaus	276	Akron, Ohio
1976	Dave Stockton	281	Bethesda, Md.
1977	Lanny Wadkins	282	Palm Beach, Cal.
1978	John Mahaffey	276	Oakmont, Pa.
1979	David Graham (Australia)	272	Oakland Hills
1980	Jack Nicklaus	274	Rochester, N.Y.
1981	Larry Nelson	273	Atlanta, Ga.
1982	Ray Floyd	272	Southern Hills
1983	Hal Sutton	274	Riviera, Cal.
1984	Lee Trevino	273	Shoal Creek

UNITED STATES MASTERS CHAMPIONSHIP

Played at the Augusta National Golf Course, Georgia

Year	Champion	Score
1934	Horton Smith	284
1935	Gene Sarazen	282
1936	Horton Smith	285
1937	Byron Nelson	283
1938	Henry Picard	285
1939	Ralph Guldahl	279
1940	Jimmy Demaret	280
1941	Craig Wood	280
1942	Byron Nelson	280
1943–45	*No championship due to the war*	
1946	Herman Keiser	282
1947	Jimmy Demaret	281
1948	Claude Harmon	279
1949	Sam Snead	283
1950	Jimmy Demaret	283
1951	Ben Hogan	280
1952	Sam Snead	286
1953	Ben Hogan	274
1954	Sam Snead	289
1955	Cary Middlecoff	279
1956	Jack Burke	289
1957	Doug Ford	283
1958	Arnold Palmer	284
1959	Art Wall	284
1960	Arnold Palmer	282
1961	Gary Player (South Africa)	280
1962	Arnold Palmer	280
1963	Jack Nicklaus	286
1964	Arnold Palmer	276
1965	Jack Nicklaus	271
1966	Jack Nicklaus	288
1967	Gay Brewer	280
1968	Bob Goalby	277
1969	George Archer	281
1970	Billy Casper	279
1971	Charles Coody	279
1972	Jack Nicklaus	286
1973	Tommy Aaron	283
1974	Gary Player (South Africa)	278

Year	Champion	Score
1975	Jack Nicklaus	276
1976	Ray Floyd	271
1977	Tom Watson	276
1978	Gary Player (South Africa)	277
1979	Fuzzy Zoeller	280
1980	Severiano Ballesteros (Spain)	275
1981	Tom Watson	280
1982	Craig Stadler	284
1983	Severiano Ballesteros (Spain)	280
1984	Ben Crenshaw	277
1985	Bernhard Langer (West Germany)	282